The Key to Good Fortune:
Refining Your Spirit

The Key to Good Fortune: Refining Your Spirit

(The Heavenly Way for All People)

by
Taoist Master
Ni, Hua-Ching

The Shrine of the Eternal Breath of Tao
College of Tao and Traditional Chinese Healing
LOS ANGELES

Acknowledgement: Thanks and appreciation to Janet DeCourtney and Frank Gibson and the students of the Center for Taoist Arts for assistance in typing, proofreading and editing this book.

The Shrine of the Eternal Breath of Tao, Malibu, California 90265
College of Tao and Traditional Chinese Healing, 117 Stonehaven Way
Los Angeles, California 90049

Dedicated to the sincere seeker
of personal spiritual growth
and the truth of eternal life

To female readers,

According to Taoist teaching, male and female are equally important in the natural sphere. This is seen in the diagram of Tai Chi. Thus, discrimination is not practiced in our tradition. All my work is dedicated to both genders of human people.

Wherever possible, constructions using masculine pronouns to represent both sexes are avoided; where they occur, we ask your tolerance and spiritual understanding. We hope that you will take the essence of my teaching and overlook the superficiality of language. Gender discrimination is inherent in English; ancient Chinese pronouns do not have differences of gender. I wish for all of your achievement above the level of language or gender.

Thank you, H. C. Ni

CONTENTS

Prelude

"Tao is the destination of all religions and spiritual effort, yet it leaves behind all religions just like the clothing of different seasons and different places. Tao is the goal of serious science, yet it leaves behind all sciences as partial and temporal descriptions of the Integral Truth.

"The teaching of Tao includes all religious subjects, yet it is not on the same level as religions. Its breadth and depth go far beyond the limits of religion. The teaching of Tao serves people's lives as religions do, yet it transcends all religions and contains the essence of all religions.

"The teaching of Tao is not like any of the sciences. It transcends the level of any single subject of science.

"The teaching of Tao is the master teaching of all. However, it does not mean that the teaching relies on a master. It means the teaching of Tao is like a master key which can unlock all doors leading to the Integral Truth. It teaches or shows the truth directly. It does not stay on the emotional surface of life or remain at the level of thought or of belief. Neither does it stay on the intellectual level of life, maintaining skepticism and endlessly searching. The teaching of Tao presents the core of the subtle truth and helps you to reach it yourself."

Part I

The Key to Good Fortune
Is Spiritual Improvement

The Key to Good Fortune
Is Spiritual Improvement

Introduction

This book contains three important treatises which I have taken from the important ancient teaching of the Taoist tradition. These three treatises are the main guidance for a mature and healthy life from a tradition many thousands of years old. They are the key to good fortune for individual people and the entire human society.

People may spend a lifetime looking for the truth of life. People may be controlled by the false disciplines of immature religious cults or prejudicial social principles and learn nothing truthful. People may sacrifice their own lives before they really reach the truth. All of these tragic facts exist. But, with an open mind, ready hand, and willing heart, a door of many thousands of blessings may open widely to welcome you. This door leads to a healthy, well-balanced and mature life - a life of self-awareness and eternity.

Of these treatises, I am merely the interpreter and elucidator. As I know, the truth cannot be written. Words are merely used as descriptions for the truth. These three treatises were evidently passed down by ageless, high divinities. I am just a student of the Truth and was fortunate enough to receive this precious guidance when I was young. But to recognize the truth - to completely subject oneself to the total truth - takes a much longer time to achieve.

Only fifty years ago, almost every village and family in China received these treatises as their basic education. It was the teaching of my forefathers. In 1949, Chinese communism started to control China. Some intellectual and revolutionary leaders thought that with this guidance as a foundation, China could never withstand the aggressive international world. My father was attacked for teaching these truths. Normalcy of life was lost in the rebellion against the old truth. The new leaders hardly saw the spiritual value in this teaching. Selfish leaders and shallow-sighted people of influence did not have a chance to review the whole truth of life before they perished.

In many generations, especially this one, people do not seek the truth, but instead seek to destroy or alter it. Can this be spiritually successful? The answer is "never." Truth is truth. For something to be recognized as truth, it must be time-tested and verified. Truth never applies only to one race; it is universal. Truth cannot successfully be rebelled against or destroyed. Truth is always unattached to time and space. It cannot be escaped; this is why it is truth. I was offered an opportunity to cultivate, live with and enjoy the truth. Once you receive it, you too shall look at it, work on it, live with it and endlessly enjoy it.

That is the purpose of this book. There is no magical performance which promotes the recognition of truth. The power of magic is short-lived. Even all great masters cease their performance. But truth and being truthful live forever.

This is the way of Heaven and the way to reconnect yourself with the Divine Nature. It enables you to awaken yourself to be able to recognize all human mistakes and to understand the danger of all negative influences. This is the way to become strong enough to withstand all enslavements.

It is important to know the truth, yet it is more important to use the truth to enrich your life and enforce your being. Truth vitalizes your root. False beliefs only serve to polish the leaves of your own life's tree. Not every person who wears a solemn robe is a spiritual teacher.

The truth teaches the perpetual way. False beliefs cause a person's life to be consumed by images or ideas. This book does not recommend anything of that sort. It only recommends the normal, perpetual flow of energy through life's channel. The rotation of the earth continues endlessly, as does the change of seasons. This is why the good flow of life is the Heavenly Way.

"Tai Shan Kan Yin Pien"
The Truth of Life
Is the Law of Spiritual Correspondence
Internally and Externally

The Ageless Truth says, "Calamities and blessings do not come through any definite, distinguishable doors but of their own accord; it is each person who invites them for oneself."

The subtle response of universal energy to one's mind and behavior is not usually recognized as the reason for calamities or blessings. Yet the accuracy of energy correspondence always occurs to people. Some of the ancients called the law of energy correspondence as the law of retribution. Whatever name used, it means that whatever a person gives out, he also receives. In fact, the quality and quantity of a person's life is totally affected or changed by the way a person thinks or behaves.

The result of good and evil thought and behavior is as inevitable as a shadow which accompany one's body. People bear the marks of crimes and sins on their auras unless personal reformation has occurred. The aura is a person's energy field that consists of one's spiritual reality. People carry their own spiritual reality with them, and the external world responds with corresponding energy. The response from the subtle realm to a person's aura is as exact as if a spiritual being were keeping records of one's evil deeds, and determining punishment according to the seriousness of the transgressions. Furthermore, there actually are spiritual beings who roam above people's heads and quietly watch them. Thus, through the energy response from the subtle realm and from the watchful spiritual beings, people receive either help and assistance or punishment and suffering. There are also evil spirits who come to reside inside a person's body if the growth of evil within them has increased to a certain amount.

Evil thoughts, behavior and energy destroy the normalcy of life. When the normal standard of life is destroyed, one's health becomes poor and one's spirit becomes wasted. One often meets with sorrow and misery, and is disliked by most people. A person of sorrow and misery is not openly welcomed by others. Punishments and calamities in all different forms pursue this person; good luck and joy shun this person and evil energy rays do this person harm. All enjoyment is stripped off; the enjoyment turns out to be poison. When the opportunity of life is exhausted, the person will die rather than having an opportunity to attain immortal spiritual life. Thus, those who seek an everlasting good life must first avoid all evil things.

How can a person keep watch on one's own spirit to increase the good and avoid evil? If your actions are appropriate, correct and good, proceed with them. To avoid evil, withdraw your energy or yourself immediately from any bad situation or one that violates the Way. Do not tread evil paths. Do nothing shameful even in private. Sometimes withdrawing from personal bad habits, evil or dangerous situations or harmful people is not easy, but consistently doing so will eventually bring its reward. Sometimes it is better to be alone than in a wrong place.

Increase the good on oneself by accumulating virtue and amass spiritual merit by thinking good thoughts and doing good deeds. Have a compassionate heart toward all creatures. Be loyal to the real authority of life, which is the spiritual energy of your life. Be filial to your parents, friendly to your younger brothers and sisters, and respectful to your older brothers and sisters. Always fulfill your share; set no demands on either family or group life but see what you can offer to others. Cultivate yourself; this will bring forth good influences on others. Be compassionate to orphans and sympathetic to the old and widowed. Respect the old and cherish the young. Assist those in need and save those in danger. Do not unreasonably hurt any living creature.

To increase your good thoughts and avoid evil ones, grieve at the misfortune of others and rejoice in their good fortune. Understand the bad tendencies or weaknesses of others and rejoice in their progress, good qualities and strengths. Regard the gains of others as your own gain, and the losses of others as your own loss. Do not publicize or talk about the shortcomings of others nor boast of your own superiorities. Yield and graciously give whatever is reasonable and necessary to meet any situation that arises, but take little from others or from situations. Accept scolding, humiliation or insult without complaint. Accept favor or good fortune with a sense of appreciation. Be kind in giving and expect no repayment.

These are general guidelines that may point you in the right direction. Each person must find one's own appropriate and safe way to extend personal good nature and kindness to the surroundings and the world. Each person does it differently depending on life station and situation. Each person must be true to the goodness of one's own natural gifts and talents rather than look to imitate outside examples.

The benefits of extending the kindness of personal good nature are great. One who is good is respected by people. People of righteousness and peaceful energy find that happiness and wealth will follow them, all evil things will shun them, and spiritual beings will help protect them. The person may even become an immortal or a god.

It is traditional spiritual knowledge that one who seeks to become a divine immortal needs to fulfill 3,000 subtle, virtuous deeds. One who seeks to become happy and lead a long life on earth needs to perform 300 - 1200 good deeds. The highest of all the good deeds is to promote harmony and peace among all people and dissolving the crisis of the burst of war with massive killing. This is true whether it is a war between nations or between two individuals.

The worst of all evil behavior is aggression or starting a war just for fulfilling personal ambition. This type of leader will be punished by righteous force.

The subtle law exists everywhere in the universe. The subtle law has no words and is expressed by subtle signs and signals. A mind which is quiet, calm and objective can read them to know whether it is correct to go ahead to engage in or undertake something of interest. However, there are people of ambition who blindly search for success through all kinds of adventure. People of adventure usually miss the signals and end up with trouble or a mess. Learning to read the subtle law is the most important learning for all sagely people who value peace and happiness in their lives more than blind adventure in human society and the agony of hidden failure.

All achieved ones in Tao know that they can best accomplish their own lives by promoting a harmonious, peaceful and healthy world. To achieve this, the approach of promoting mutual understanding among all human people is an effective practice and a spiritual cultivation.

Conversely, if one acts contrary to righteousness or behaves improperly; if one is insatiably covetous and greedy and swears to seek vindication for one's own shame; if one loves liquor or drugs and becomes rude, weak and disorderly; if one is angry and quarrelsome with people; if one is not in harmony with other people; if one treats the spirits of one's ancestors with disrespect; if one is unfaithful towards family, duties, or occupation; if one is occupied with what is not beneficial to either oneself or others; if one cherishes a disloyal heart; if one curses oneself and others or is partial in one's love and projects hatred; if one disrespects the source of one's food and drink and abuses it; if one kills babies, misuses abortions or commits acts of secret depravity; if one does not remain peaceful and quiet at the beginning and end of the day, month and year; if one violates the natural energy field corresponding with the directions such as in how a house is built, or violates seasonal cycles in ways such as planting in the wrong season or engaging in unusual activities; if one disrespects the sacredness of one's home or body, or if one disrespects the sacredness of natural energy sources such as the sun, moon and stars; if one oppresses inferiors and claims credit for it; if one courts superiors by gratifying their evil desires; if one broods over resentments; if one knows one's faults and does not work to change them or knows what is good and does not do it; if one blames another person for one's own mistakes; if one kills without any proper reasons; if one commits these or similar crimes, errors or infractions, the Subtle Arbiter of Destiny within and without one's being will, according to the seriousness of the crime, devitalize the person's life, devastate the person's efforts, and deprive him of reaping any good harvest that otherwise might have come to him. If death does not occur to these people, then for the current as well as future generations and lives, they and their families will continue to be plagued with evil.

Moreover, if a person wrongly seizes another's property, that person, or the person's spouse, children, or other members of the family, shall all be held responsible. This is sometimes true on the visible level of human law and justice, but it is also true on the invisible level of spirit. The expiation or compensation is proportionate to the wrongdoing. If the wrongdoer or his family do not die, then there will be what seems like punishment in the form of disasters from water, fire, thieves, loss of property or position, illness or war. This kind of punishment also applies in situations involving the incorrect seizure of high positions and social power. The problems of one's surroundings or living environment may be the focal point of individual spiritual problems.

One who kills people unjustly or puts weapons into the hands of others will find that those others will eventually turn on him and he will be killed by those weapons. One who seizes property or power unrighteously is like the one who relieves hunger with spoiled food or quenches thirst with poisoned wine. Fullness will last only momentarily; death will inevitably follow.

A certain amount of true mistake-making is allowed by the subtle law. A person is allowed to learn. However, if a person continues to do things with bad or selfish intent or fails to correct one's errors, retribution may occur. This is why it is said, "The net of Heaven and the meshes of justice are loose but never miss."

There are many who do evil deeds and later repent of their own accord and correct their behavior and thoughts. By refraining from doing any further evil and earnestly practicing good thoughts, words and deeds, over time, one will surely obtain good fortune. This is what is called spiritual transformation or salvation. It manifests by changing the calamities of one's life into blessings through spiritual improvement.

Improvement occurs not only on the level of action but also in thought. He who thinks good, even before the good is accomplished, will find good spirits helping him. Conversely, he who thinks evil, even before the evil is done, will find that the bad spirits are together with him.

Therefore, the person of good fortune speaks good, sees good, and does good. Every day, if one realizes these three kinds of goodness, at the end of three years, one's good being will invite blessings and Heaven will come to help. The time period of three years is not fixed or rigid, but that is maybe an average time that sincere, constant and dedicated practice can turn a person's life around.

The person of evil fortune speaks evil, sees evil and does evil. If every day one has these three kinds of evil, at the end of three years, one's evil being invites calamities, and Heaven departs from this person. The spiritual realm is consistent in how it operates. Good or evil result depend upon the intent of the person.

Most people who are on a spiritual path are not evil people but just have a few things to work out and further evolution to accomplish.

Truthful words may not be beautiful to hear, but beautiful words may not always be helpful to people in their lives. This is not beautiful poetry or an eloquent essay. Neither is it a graceful work of literature or ornamental knowledge. But it is the plain truth of life. Here it is earnestly stated.

The Way of Heaven - and "Yin Jyh Wen" The Silent Way of Blessing

The following work was written by a Taoist achieved one whose name was Chahng O. "Yin Jyh Wen" and the treatises reveal the truth that "Good works done in secret will be rewarded by Heaven," or "Heaven secretly blesses good people." In truth, good works and a good life are a direct correlation and are enjoyed by people of good spirituality. Chahng O lived as a recluse after serving as a royal official of the Tang dynasty (620-950 A.D.) His moral power had a tremendous unconscious influence on the Chinese people.

Chahng O realized the Heavenly Way. He extended his power to protect people of learning, especially in art and literature. He left behind the sole document about personal experiences of soul evolution through many generations.

As Chapter 54 of the *Tao Teh Ching* (or The Sacred Book of the Integral Way) says, "The well-built cannot be removed. The firmly held cannot slip away. The one who builds himself with virtue will be honored by generations to come." The people of Shu, where Chahng O lived, showed great respect for him and built a temple in his name after he died. Numerous elegant, towering pavilions were built as temples and memorials in almost every city in China. Descendants have long made sacrifices to Chahng O. (In Taoism, life and death are considered mere "signs" of a great transformation.)

"The Silent Way of Blessing"

The Sacred Scripture by Chahng O:

"For seventeen generations, I have incarnated as a man of superior position and I have never oppressed people or my subordinates. I have saved people from misfortune, helped people in need, shown pity to orphans and forgiven people for their mistakes. I have extensively practiced the subtle virtue of doing good deeds without requiring anything in return. In this way, I became attuned to the Heavenly Way.

If you can set your mind on things as I have, then Heaven will surely bestow blessings upon you. Therefore, here are the suggestions I give to you:

Whosoever wants to expand his field of happiness must rely on his own inner moral nature.

Do good work at all times and secretly practice many meritorious deeds.

Benefit living creatures and human beings by cultivating goodness and happiness.

Be honest and straightforward, and on behalf of Heaven, promote moral reform for yourself and others.

Be compassionate and merciful, and for the sake of human love, serve people.

Be faithful to your leader and serve your parents with maturity.

Be respectful toward elders and truthful with friends.

Let some worship the Three Pure Ones - Yi, Shi, and Vi - and revere the divine subtle rays of the highest sphere of the universe; let others bow before various statues and recite from different sacred books. These ways are merely expressions of the different levels of the evolving human spirit and are the reality of personal growth.

Repay the kindness that has been bestowed upon you by Heaven, earth, parents and society.

Help people in distress. Free people from danger as you would free a bird from a net.

Be compassionate to orphans and kind to widows. Respect the aged and have pity for the poor and the poor in spirit. Collect food and clothing to relieve those who are hungry and cold. Be sure you are well-prepared when you travel and, especially on your spiritual journey, be independent.

Give away coffins so the dead among the poor will not be exposed. Also have a coffin for yourself in which to bury your own ego and the past.

If your own family is well provided for, extend a helping hand to relatives. If the harvest fails, help your neighbors and friends. Also, do not continue to hold grudges against enemies of days gone by. Extend a hand to them also.

Let measure and scales be accurate, and do not give less when selling or take more when buying. Above all, have accurate scales for your virtues, too.

Treat your employees with fairness and consideration. Why should you be severe when disciplining and harsh with your demands? Try this behavior on yourself first!

Write and publish sacred scriptures, but realize that the best is not said with words, but with subtle virtue.

Build and repair temples and shrines, and when doing so, do not neglect the temple and shrine within yourself.

Distribute herbs for medicine in order to alleviate suffering of the sick. In all of your actions, be aware of your own sick-mindedness.

Offer tea and water to relive distress from thirst and use them to replace liquors and drugs that cause sickness.

Keep your diet primarily vegetarian.

Abstain from taking life by your own hand or at your command; it is not permissible for mankind to slaughter the lives of others.

Whenever taking a step, watch for ants and insects, lest you hurt one of them. If the privileged in life are determined by size, then camels should ride on humans!

Prohibit the building of fires outside, lest insects be killed; do not set woods or forests ablaze. Also do not set "fire" among people.

Have a light that illuminates the outside of your house at night so that visitors will not stumble. Have a light to guide your own life, especially through those dark moments.

Build boats to ferry people across rivers. (This was the ancient practice.) Be a "ferry" for those who are unable to cross life's troubled waters.

Do not go into the woods to catch birds in nets nor to the waters to trap fish. Do not set nets of greed or aggression for yourself. Instead, destroy all poisonous motives within you.

Do not butcher the ox that plows your fields. (This was ancient practice. It also means to treat your helpers fairly.)

Do not throw away your writing or let paper be scattered on the ground; also respect the writing of others.

Do not scheme for other property or neglect the property within yourself.

Do not envy the skills or abilities of others, but sharpen your own in order to better serve people.

Do not sexually harm the spouse or children of others. Sexual violation only results in self-destruction and has no benefit.

Do not initiate litigation. Righteousness can only be found by the inspection of one's innermost self.

Do not injure the reputation or interest of others. This behavior injures your own virtue and reflects your own insufficient character.

Do not destroy marriages. This creates broken hearts for children.

Do not, on account of personal enmity, create disharmony between brothers and sisters. Do not, because of small profits, cause parents and their children to quarrel. Keep yourself outside the families of others. Be the spectator to worldly competition.

Do not misuse your power to disgrace the good and the law-abiding. This is a spiritual flaw.

Do not become a dictator or a tyrant. Dictatorship is the fact of spiritual undevelopment. If you are a leader, work to find the balance among differences and be open to accepting good advance from any source.

Do not support a dictator or a tyrant. Supporting tyranny is the fact of spiritual inferiority. Give your support to leaders of open and broad principles; if none exist, become one yourself or withdraw from activity.

Do not join social groups or movements which hold prejudice. Prejudice is mental and spiritual uncleanliness. Join people for the good common goal of mutual spiritual help or development.

Do not become the source of trouble for other people or society. Being a source of trouble is spiritual carelessness. Be alert and see what you can do to help or learn a skill so that you can be helpful. The majority of people are the children of Heaven. They need good care, good guidance and inspiration from spiritual people who prepare themselves to have something truly nice to offer.

Do not gather people or use public force to achieve your personal ambition. Using other people or their property shows spiritual poverty. Work hard and achieve your goals through your own effort.

Do not become a leader of emotional hatred or bias. This is a spiritual defect. If you are a leader, constantly examine your motives. Make no hasty moves or lose your rationality.

Do not join action out of emotional or immoral reason. This shows spiritual shortness. Action of any kind should be taken only after careful thought and consideration to be sure it will be beneficial to all concerned.

Do not force people to yield to you, give you things or agree with what you want. This is barbaric spiritual behavior and those people are damaged by you. If you cannot obtain what you need through upright means, change your plans or direction.

Do not fan a social riot. Find calmer ways to improve situations.

Do not adopt any ideology without truly experimenting to test its validity. This shows spiritual unclarity. It is better to be silent and have a broad humanistic attitude than to find out later that what you believed was good actually hurt yourself and others.

Do not follow or choose what people believe without personal objective examination. This shows spiritual negligence. Read and experience widely to learn what is truthful. Choose something that meets your stage of growth, but do not commit yourself to anything that might stop your further growth.

Do not create a social force for the purpose of injustice. Guard yourself from the evil of other people or the government. Keep your actions in a positive direction; do not let them focus on negativity, even to fight something wrong.

Respect and guard two most important assets belonging to you and to all other people. They are the natural rights of human people and the freedom that provides for a broad spiritual development.

To refuse cooperation with any unjust force, retreat from any place where darkness strongly dominates. It is better to start a new life somewhere else than to live with injustice, fear and danger.

Always have a clear idea and correct understanding about what you are doing and your work. Do not accept a job of immorality or cause trouble for someone else for high payment. Do not refuse a job of moral significance or public spirited meaning for low payment.

Do not use your wealth to oppress the poor and needy. Instead, offer them opportunities for survival and better living.

Be close to, and friendly with, the good; this will improve your own moral character. Keep a distance from the bad; this will help protect you from imminent danger. Watch your mind as you defend yourself from robbers and cheaters.

Conceal people's vices but proclaim their virtues, lest you misjudge them.

Do not say "yes" with your mouth and "no" with your heart. Always keep your mouth and heart in accord with each other.

Cut brambles and thorns that obstruct the road. Remove bricks and stones that lie in the path. This practice will help remove obstacles in your future.

Repair the roads that have been rough for years, since they, too, help to smooth your own life's road.

Build bridges over which thousands of people may travel. (This was an ancient practice.) Be a "bridge" for people trying to reach the Pure Realm.

Leave moral instruction so that others can correct their faults. More importantly, leave your subtle virtuous merits for the generations to come.

Donate money to help others complete their good deeds. By doing this, you actually make your own virtues complete.

Follow the way of Heaven in your life. Listen to, and obey, what your heart says in all your actions.

Admire the ancient integral model of sages to the extent that you see them while eating your meal or looking at anything or anyone.

Be so clear in conscience that when you sleep alone, you are not ashamed before your bed; and when you walk alone, you are not ashamed before your own shadow. In this way, you are totally responsible for your own being.

Refrain from doing evil, but earnestly do good deeds. This is the highest doctrine of all good religions. Thus, there will never be any ill influences upon you, and you will always be protected by good and auspicious spirits.

If you do some or all of these things, immediate reward will come to you, and later rewards will reach your posterity. A hundred blessings will come to you like a chariot pulled by rushing horses; a thousand fortunes will surround you like auspicious clouds gathering above.

All these things come through the silent way of blessing as I have revealed to you.

Master Ni's Commentary:
"Tai Shan Kan Yin Pien" and "Yin Jyh Wen"

I

The responsiveness of the mind and one's behavior play a decisive role in one's personal fortune. The natural energy formation of each individual is fundamental in this regard. To a great extent, one's thoughts and actions comprise much of one's energy formation. One's energy formation is physical, too, but not entirely.

Here is a physical example for you to understand how each person must be true to one's own nature. A duck has a long neck but short legs. This is its natural formation. One could not expect to cut off a portion of the duck's long neck and use it to lengthen its legs and thus have a more "desirable" duck. As for an individual's or a family's fortune, there are always some things longer and some things shorter.

However, the process of nature is always evolving and transforming, especially in human life. The long process of the formation of individual human life happens during many lifetimes. (This is actually the meaning of "evolution.") Therefore, in every moment, we are forming or reforming ourselves, and the environment reacts to what and how we are forming.

As we go through our day, do we fit the spiritual environment? Does the subtle reformation of the spiritual environment suit us (such as, is there a spot of spiritual low energy or a perch for evil energy that we need to avoid)? This means we need to check whether we fit the environment well. Each environment is constantly reforming itself, and some places devolve to become places of low spiritual energy or evil energy. Personal tension causes tension in the environment; a person's self-dissolution causes dissolution of the blocks in the subtle environment. The former is called negative creativity and the later, positive creativity.

In life, harmony or balance is the highest virtue. Each individual being is responsible for every moment of one's being. Personal destiny is just the shadow of one's mind or the pattern of one's dreams.

Spiritual education is higher than the moral education of the cultural sphere because it comes from the good, inner nature of a person. Yet, spirituality and morality cannot be divided in a general sense. A spiritual person is naturally a moral person. However, a moral person is not necessarily a person of high spiritual achievement, because sometimes morality is learned intellectually from external sources or by imitation rather than being a part of one's own goodness.

On the spiritual level, high morality rests on the attainment of high spiritual awareness. This is natural morality. Natural morality rebukes the imitation of morality. This imitation is mockery; it is not real. If things are not real, how can they be natural?

To the vast human society, moral education is not natural, but its source is from the natural truth. Thus, it can be valued and encouraged. The pursuit of spiritual growth cannot be separated from the growth of individual life. On a deep spiritual basis, spiritual growth is amoral, which means that it is neither moral nor immoral. The sense of morality is transcended on the spiritual level. This may astonish the ordinary mind! But spiritual growth is still moral when it involves the sphere of yin and yang.

In the long run, human life cannot escape the moral way. To a highly achieved spiritual person, being moral exists every moment; it cannot be evaded. The practice of following Tao in one's life thus implies living in a natural moral way. The natural moral way is a state of high spiritual energy rather than a social code of educated morality. The social code is what you learn to accommodate. Spiritual morality means natural expression without decorating yourself.

The foundation of natural morality is not the erroneous cultural or religious morality. For example, with educated morality, in places where weapons are kept, many people are asked to kill (as in wars) because others may be different.

However, natural morality does not support killing people just because their backgrounds are different.

Natural morality is spiritual integration; divine immortality is the fruit one reaps by engaging in a lifetime process of cultivation. As we move into our own deep sense of natural morality, we need to discard all cultural and religious fabrications and conceptions. They are merely expressions limited by time, race and the spiritual status of their leaders. Some naturally moral people hold the truth of life without even knowing anything about cultural and religious morality or concepts. We hold a great appreciation for natural morality, for it expresses how we are shaped and formed as real beings in any time, in any space, and in any lifetime.

The above treatise is known as "Tai Shan Kan Yin Pien" which was elucidated as the Subtle Law of the Universe and translated into English in my book, *Tao, the Subtle Universal Law and the Integral Way of Life*. Both original works, "Tai Shan Kan Yin Pien" and "Yin Jyh Wen" can be found in any rural village in China, although there may only be a few books which exist in the whole town. Millions of copies have been distributed over the years by people of good will. This book has been the deep-rooted religious and spiritual education for the majority of Chinese people.

II

These two pieces of writing mainly teach how to discern good from bad, right from wrong and virtue from evil. They also teach you how to project your mind. Your mind makes all good and bad things happen on a general level. However, sometimes things happen that are related to the more subtle sphere of your mind, such as subconscious images, projections, or unconscious self-suggestions. These things may strongly influence you without actually coming to the surface of your self-knowing. This is why it is good practice to take some time every seven days to establish a self-inspection to figure out what subtle things are bothering you. It is similar to a technician checking out whether a valuable and delicate piece of equipment needs to be repaired or mended. For a person, it is like a general tune-up in which you examine yourself psychologically, emotionally, mentally and spiritually.

You examine the issues and conflicts in yourself and in your life to see what you can improve. It is much more valuable than doing something wrong and causing yourself big trouble and remorse. After some time, you will not need to do it every day, but only every several months or every several years.

This is similar to taking good care of your own body. Self-care such as good diet, exercise, etc., pays off. It is far better to do routine bodily care than to wait for big trouble to happen which may or not be able to be fixed.

What we talk about here is just an example. It is not law. The subtle law is not worded; it is something that happens everywhere in all places by itself when the law of immortals and the law of souls are one. The immortals talk about it by saying that a person can meet it by following important principles, such as being balanced, being calm, being upright, etc., in order to abide with the spiritual energy. Those principles are applied in specific situations rather than being rigidly followed all the time.

To follow external rules without understanding when they are to be applied is the mistake of most religious followers. Each principle or guideline of life has a correct time and place to which it is best applied. The different rules and commandments to institute different customs really split the unity of humankind. Practically, those things, when overly extreme and irritating, are opposite to the subtle law.

The subtle law is also subtle energy. The subtle law is a term to describe how the subtle energy can be reached. This is the essence of all lives and of all of nature.

When you follow the subtle law, practically you identify with the subtle law. Even talking about the subtle law is only one way of talking about the truth of natural life. Truth is natural. Only from naturalness is there truth. If you live with the ultimate truth of naturalness, you achieve the highest freedom. This is how to achieve the undefinable Tao, undefinable path, the truth of eternity.

A Sage has no Sickness of Personality
Because of Knowing and Working on Personal Problems

According to Lao Tzu, it is valuable for each individual to know one's own problems and correct them. The following describes when a person has strayed from the original natural morality and needs to make correction in thought, speech or action. There are also some things to avoid. These things are a kind of sickness that each person needs to cure by himself.

To be moody and fussy and use others as one's victim is sick.
To be greedy and disregard righteousness is sick.
To be lascivious and ignore one's own virtue is sick.
To cling to worldly objects is sick.
To hate others and to pray for their death is sick.
To overindulge in something that one likes and to discard one's spiritual light is sick.
To defame the reputations of others and then to boast of one's own goodness is sick.
To change for one's own benefit that which has already been accepted is sick.
To rejoice in the misfortunes of others is sick.
To convert one's virtues to new, fashionable immature thoughts is sick.
To be in treacherous collusion is sick.
To pass rumors about anything is sick.
To hold a narrow view and mislead people is sick.
To make false statements is sick.
To defile the good name of others is sick.
To swindle simple people is sick.
To brag about one's own achievements is sick.
To use force, capability, and speech in a violent way is sick.
To be dualistic in thinking and unfaithful to one's true nature is sick.
To lie and cheat is sick.
To be meddlesome in the business of others is sick.
To disclose the secrets of others is sick.
To look into the activities of others without their knowledge and approval is sick.
To bewilder people so that they stumble and fall is sick.
To teach evil is sick.
To rob people of their profits is sick.
To take from others when they do not have the strength to resist is sick.
To be deceitful is sick.
To injure others with evil and crafty means is sick.

To postulate conclusions is sick.
To misappropriate and cheat is sick.
To suppress the weak and help the violent is sick.
To be hypocritical is sick.
To be untruthful in speech and insincere in thought is sick.
To bend your virtuous principles for popular interests is sick.
To be jealous of another's virtues and capabilities is sick.
To engage in extravagant talk and impure chatter is sick.
To allure and entice the naive is sick.
To use slanderous language is sick.
To seduce the young, ignorant or naive is sick.
To vilify the virtuous is sick.
To exaggerate in emotions and speech is sick.
To harshly treat those who are lost is sick.
To pride oneself on one's own intelligence and to use this
    sarcastically against others is sick.
To abuse one's own influence by suppressing others is sick.
To borrow and not return is sick.
To take pride in one's wealth is sick.
To take pride in one's honor and glory is sick.
To envy those who become prosperous is sick.
To ridicule the success of others is sick.
To please or be pleased by flattery is sick.
To take pride in one's own high virtue is sick.
To obstruct another from accomplishments is sick.
To disturb public affairs with selfish purposes is sick.
To disguise bad motives with a beautiful approach is sick.
To make people believe that one is straight when one is
    actually crooked is sick.
To insult others with what one thinks is correct is sick.
To feel that others are disgusting but to praise oneself is sick.
To think that one is superior to all others is sick.
To take credit for other people's accomplishments is sick.
To complain about one's own life is sick.
To make people believe that a fabricated story is true is sick.
To endanger others in order to acquire or preserve one's own
    security, or because one likes to behave this way, is sick.
To incite a riot is sick.
To be critical of the affairs of others, but not to practice one's
    own cultivation is sick.
To cause others to be burdensome is sick.

To take advantage of people is sick.

To use people's shortcomings for controlling them is sick.

To expect repayments for doing favors is sick.

To demand that people do you favors is sick.

To envy what others have acquired is sick.

To argue habitually is sick.

To curse animals is sick.

To use black magic is sick.

To disgrace the talents and virtues of others is sick.

To hate people or yourself because others are better than you is sick.

To take drugs or use alcohol improperly is sick.

To hold prejudices is sick.

To blame or resent others for their wrongdoing is sick.

To refuse the good advice and teachings of others is sick.

To behave recklessly is sick.

To be unreasonable is sick.

To be self-righteous is sick.

To hold skepticism toward all truth is sick.

To make fun of people who are insane and ill is sick.

To be arrogant and impolite is sick.

To disrespect people who are young or old is sick.

To adhere to an unhealthy environment is sick.

To be undutiful in one's work is sick.

To fail to take responsibility for your own safety, finances, health and life is sick.

Part II

The Key to a Better World

Chapter 1

The Key to Good Fortune of the World Is Still Spiritual Improvement of All Individuals

How long has the human race engaged in religious activity? We can trust that it started at a very early time. We can trust that religious activity is the earliest human cultural creation which arose even before any other cultural expression was formed. All civilization is the offspring of the religious activity of primitive people. Civilization is an intellectual achievement. Culture is a beautification of general life with its conditions, conceptions and internal outreach.

Let us take a bird's eye view of the history of human religious activity, with our primary focus being on the achievement of different spiritual realizations of many generations.

Religion has two possible achievements. One is to worship either many gods or one god. Most existing religions are concerned with external beliefs. They identify and name gods or deities believed to be supporters of people's lives. They also establish rituals and offerings to secure the support of those supposed external sources. For most people, worshipping is a way of looking for external spiritual help for life.

The second type of achievement came later than the first. It is centered around the discovery of the self; plainly stated, the spiritual self, because, of course, the self has many levels. This discovery came after many years of reflection and arose much later than the establishment of external religious worship. Some wise people observed and reflected that many people had naturally good lives without being overtly religious. They wondered, "What would constitute a practical direction for improving one's life? Is it enjoying more health, wealth, longevity or healthy fun, or does external religion offer an approach that brings some truthful fruit?" After their observation of people with good lives who continued to live close to nature, they concluded that those people were not lacking in character or spiritual achievement. This inspired people to conclude that the self was the path. This conclusion encouraged some people to take the way of a general good life and encouraged other people to begin their own, different search for the true self. Individuals look to the universal natural spiritual sphere for support to do this. That is how various paths were created.

Christianity, Judaism, Islam and Hinduism are all external religions. They do not look to the universal natural spiritual sphere for support. Zhan (Zen) Buddhism and the Sufi sect of Islam are examples of traditions looking for the spiritual self, instead of something external to believe in. They recognize that external spiritual reality is actually the internal spiritual self. They are internal religions. Thus, the two types of religions are internal and external.

Unfortunately, even internal religious teachings are still very much fixed to the conventional background from which the religions arose. In other words, they did not establish spiritual independence from their religious roots. There may be some specially achieved masters who have done so, but the politics of religion keep this achievement a secret from the world.

What is the correct pursuit in life and in conjunction with spiritual learning? In viewing religious teachings, the purpose of the establishment of religion, or both kinds of spiritual practice, is to decide: do you have a soul or not? Both teachings consider the basic questions: What are you living for? Are you living for a surface life or for a deeper understanding of life? If a person lives on the level of looking only for material support, he may discover that he cannot obtain all that he needs in life by himself. All life needs both material support and spiritual support. When people need external spiritual support, external religions arise, and people believe that by their offerings and prayers, they will secure the things they need.

Religious people who believe in the internal path of the self deny that benefit can be obtained by an external religious approach. Therefore, they look inwardly, after being either inspired or repulsed by external religion. They arrive at this conclusion: the external spiritual reality which people worship is actually found in the spiritual reality of one's own self.

People can usually only see or conceive of life in concrete terms, but some people wonder about the existence of the soul which is not concrete and cannot be thought about in the same way as a material object. Some religions never even discuss the soul. In other words, in religion there is not necessarily a connection between requiring people to comply with its teachings and the reality of the soul. This is why people have asked me, Is there a soul, and can the soul be saved through the religious approach?

For the most part, most people experience only their minds and emotions. Both mind and emotion are projections of life energy. The development of both will differ depending upon the person's understanding of this energy. Because the mind and emotions connect directly with life, people need to establish a new or different way of perception that frees them from the rigidity of their old life connections. Once we find a different way to handle our mind and emotions, we are much happier; it can save us or deliver us so we can immediately go to a different stage of awareness.

In different generations, the soul has been called by different names, such as the deep sense, the subconscious mind or the conscious mind, but it is still the soul. You can also call it energy; that is appropriate and correct, but there are also other specific kinds of energy besides soul energy. Just like any other energy, the soul can be scattered. There must first be convergence before scatteredness can happen. If there is no convergence, then there is no way something can be scattered. When the kind of subtle energy referred to as the soul converges, it is the soul. We will use the old term of soul; if you do not like it, you can use your own term. It just refers to a kind of energy, the spiritual energy or the soul.

On another level, this convergence of energy we call the soul is recognition. It is your mind. Whatever we believe about recognition, it is still energy. Recognition is connected with memory. Memory affects recognition and recognition affects memory. Some people know there is something more to their being besides their mind and body. Thus, they are aware that there is some kind of energy that carries recognition, memory and personality. People call it a person's nature, sensibility or sensitivity. A person who is open enough can accept another term for that nature and call it the soul.

Anybody who believes in reincarnation must admit that there must be an insistent substance that reincarnates. It is not being overly conservative to adopt the old term "soul" in an open and realistic discussion of these ideas.

Practically, how can a soul be saved? Perhaps a different approach or focus is needed from what general religion puts out as saving the soul. True spiritual growth is not a matter of saving the soul in a religious sense, but rather of developing and cultivating the soul.

The human race grew through primitive stages and looked for achievement, step by step. Despite all that achievement, even now, the soul of most individuals is neither conceptually developed nor strong enough to attain a clear vision of either external or internal reality. Most people end up confusing themselves by relying on external teachings. Relying on external teachings is a continuation of dependence, a stage to go through. If people do not correct this, they neglect their need to grow, which prevents their further development. Development of the soul is more important than relying on established beliefs.

My works are like external teachings, but they serve you differently. They are not an organized program or a social activity. They are works which stimulate your own thought and reflection about your own life and your relationship to the universe. It is appropriate to study my works. In them, you will be shown a different kind of spiritual reality. You will read that your spiritual responsibility is not to worry about the loss of the soul. Your soul will be not lost; your soul needs developing. There is no imaginary monster that will eat up your soul. There is no punishment by an external force that will cut or burn your soul. The strength of the soul is a measure of your own development. The punishment of the soul is your own undevelopment; a soul is chained or caged by undevelopment. This is why the free soul or flying soul points out the good direction for all souls, because it is the developed soul. It is my hope that my books raise questions in your mind and that you figure out the answers. This is one way that internal growth takes place.

There are many good spiritual achievements described in my books that will help you to understand the reality of the soul and see the correct way to develop your soul. You can especially learn the position of your soul in life and the value of balance. Those things cannot be neglected when you are searching for your soul and attending to its development.

In the stage of fleshly or physical life, the soul is not a single existence nor does it live outside of your body. It not only makes your body its house, it makes your life the support of its soul life.

This book tells the truth. It is the direct, internal truth, the result of many generations of people's searching. For a long time nobody had a clear understanding; perhaps sometimes clarity was reached, then the next moment, perhaps it was lost again in the confusion of external teaching or reference. You may wish to consider this discussion a conclusion to all the generations' different spiritual approaches in reaching the truth. But it is not a conclusion, it is an achievement. With this achievement as a benchmark, you can reflect back on the level of worldly teaching.

Chapter 2

Heavenly Way for All People

It is not mere imagination that a better world can be reached through the spiritual improvement of all individuals, races and nations. The Heavenly Way which is the way to spiritual improvement was the teaching of Fu Shi, Shen Nung, the Yellow Emperor, Niao, Shun, Lao Tzu and Mo Tzu. The teaching of the Heavenly Way shows the way to reach Heaven.

Many people talk about Heaven or God in a conventional way as something else or somewhere else, not as themselves or during the time when they live. That type of thought about Heaven was somebody's psychological projection, or even self-deception. Have you ever asked anybody if they have been to a place called Heaven? I would like to give you the opportunity to answer the question, "Have you been in Heaven?" You would simply tell me, "No." If I ask you, "What is Heaven like?" you would perhaps assure me that Heaven is a place away from the world where you feel wonderful, where there is no trouble, not even a little. You enjoy peacefulness and everything you like in that place, and it is really happy. This might be your answer.

However, the Heavenly Way that we talk about in the Tradition of Tao is different. The Heavenly Way starts from where you are and what you are. It is not far away, because it starts from you. However, it is also not near if you do not make it one of your goals and work for it. It is a direction of life. It is also a destination. Thus, it is a spiritual reality in which the direction is in the destination and the destination is in the direction. It is not an ideology. It is the fulfillment of a natural, healthy life.

If you still ask, "Where is Heaven?" I would like to answer you again even more earnestly. It is within you. There is a way to get there. However, it is an individual matter, so I think we need to discuss our own spiritual reality openly, but not discuss the reality of other people. We really cannot accurately judge from appearances or know about other people and how they relate to Heaven.

First, we must clearly understand that Heaven is not a place apart from this world. Heaven can be experienced in any time or place that has all wonderful healthy supportive energy. Practically, Heaven can happen in any person or any group of people. When people grow to the stage of knowing how Heaven is created, they will have Heavenly life. If there is no Heaven in our lives, our lives are not worthy.

In your life experience, usually no one asks you if you wish to ascend to Heaven except when the clergy of a church asks you to make a donation.

Do you wish to create Heaven on earth? No, you cannot create a paradise for everyone. What you can do is to cultivate Heaven within yourself. A person who has a Heaven within is usually a person who has a Heaven outside, too.

On many occasions, the undualistic Heavenly way recognizes that the original human nature is Heavenly nature. The original human nature and Heaven are not two different things. When this human or Heavenly nature is obstructed and cannot be expressed, it means there is a problem or struggle. It is true that nobody lives in the world and experiences a life of no problems. However, coping with problems means that once you receive a bad experience, you change yourself to be able to better cope with the situation if it happens again. You do not hold grudges against others but keep your positive, Heavenly energy alive in your life. Unfortunately, some people are stubborn, so when the Heavenly energy within them is blocked, rather than change, they become cruel, greedy, scheming or violent. If they become like that and stay that way, their Heavenly energy totally dies. A person who does not extend one's Heavenly energy lives in hell. Hell is where and when people let their Heavenly energy be blocked within and do not express it. Hell is not a place of fire burning after death, as religions so often portray it.

Some people of purity leave their families to go learn about the world when they are young. Slowly they build their independence. How do they grow after that? Basically, by carrying that pure Heavenly energy with them and using it all the time. They have been honorable people, not thieves or beggars. They have been people working in small jobs or big jobs. They have given all kinds of service to others in their practical daily lives using skills developed by their human ancestors or themselves.

Life experience is not always like a smooth ocean. Sometimes it is rough because the world is rough. During our generation, there have been several different wars, one after another.

Heavenly people do not like wars. Unfortunately, they sometimes suffer from wars. Those people who are Heavenly are not harmful people. They do not look at what is in other people's pockets, nor do they have any interest in stealing other people's belongings, skills, lives or anything else. They help others when they can.

The world's people are mixed. Good people are Heavenly people. But whether a person is a good person or not cannot be totally decided by us. This is why rather than trying to figure out other people, a better way to use our energy is to develop and improve ourselves. That will help to make our way smooth.

We might say that about 60% of the people we meet are good people. This tells us that most people are harmless people. There are poisonous and harmful people, too. You may ask me, have you ever been cheated, tricked, wronged, robbed or misunderstood? Yes, I have been. However, I am on the Heavenly Way. It is an important goal to stay on the Heavenly Way and not be influenced or changed by people whose backgrounds and perceptions are different.

There are good people in almost every society. However, good people always seem to be on the side being persecuted in an unnatural society, such as those living under the rule of communism. Bad people are always on the side of persecuting others. Although the good suffer, they live longer and with greater psychological peace than the beasts with sharp teeth and sharp jaws.

If Heaven were somewhere apart from this world, then there would be no goodness or help in life. Heaven must be in your home and in your being. Then you will enjoy a good life, good support and good growth. When Heaven is found in your office, then your office will be productive and effective.

Heaven must be found on streets, highways, freeways and everywhere, otherwise Heaven is not real.

Real Heaven is not a psychological projection, expectation or hope. Heaven is our personal discipline and cultivation. That is how to achieve Heaven, to build the way to reach Heaven; otherwise, Heaven is just like a carrot on a stick in front of the donkey and is of no use. When you learn to discipline yourself and cultivate your energy, you change yourself to be a better person. When you are a better person, you will discover that good people become interested in you and bad people stay away because they do not enjoy themselves around you any more. This is helpful in the area of personal relationships, because when you become a loving, giving person to other people, one of two things may happen. One thing is that your existing relationship with girlfriend, boyfriend, partner or spouse will either begin to change positively (if the person is already a loving person or begins to change too) or deteriorate due to their own wish (if they are not ready for increased goodness and energy.) The second thing is that if your relationship has dropped away or you are not in a relationship, you may find yourself becoming involved with a good, loving person. This is called the law of spiritual correspondence. It means that energy attracts corresponding energy. Being supportive and friendly is Heaven.

Heaven can be built by tolerance, patience and understanding for those to whom you are related, such as family members, colleagues, fellow students and others. If you lose patience, you may cause some friction, and a small disagreement may turn out to be a war. Lack of patience makes things destructive; a more relaxed attitude brings constructive measures.

What is the purpose of religions? Their purpose may have originally been to bring people to an understanding of the real Heaven, but the original message has been distorted by people who have not understood it. Unfortunately, their teachings have been used for wrong reasons and have created the opposite of Heaven, such as hatred and prejudice among people. If they create prejudice, many people are sacrificed or sacrifice their Heaven for prejudice and hatred in wars with people of different beliefs. That is not Heaven; it is hell. Can you be aware of that?

The teaching of Tao, at the spiritual level, mostly concentrates on the Heavenly Way. The teaching is the Heavenly Way. By following the guidance contained in this book, you may reach Heaven right away.

If you have already realized Heaven in your life, then you are Heaven. Then the Heavenly way is a description of the real you. If you are not realizing Heaven in your life now, then temporarily your Heavenly energy is blocked. The obstruction can be moved with your own help so that your good nature can extend out to the world.

First, extend your Heavenly energy in the right circumstances to the people in your surroundings. Once you show your Heavenly energy, if you have enough patience, your surroundings will turn out to be Heaven. Heaven is like a wonderful party, except without the junk food and the junk soft drinks - instead with good food and drinks. It is a party so wonderful; it is never tiring to talk to each other or join in union with each other.

I have said that Heaven is within you. After the internal Heaven becomes a part of you, your experience of the world will change to become a kind of Heaven, too. We can describe the qualities of the external Heaven in a different way: Heaven has its purpose. Heaven has its shape. What is the purpose of Heaven? It is to provide a good, natural, healthy, free environment for all people. Heaven has a shape. What is its shape? It is shaped by many good people coming together, meeting each other, helping each other and working things out by mature help. Thus, Heaven is not an escape like a hiding place where people can hide from the world. If you escape your life, you escape Heaven, and you go somewhere else. You will find Heaven if you decide to.

For example, when some people are at school, they are troubled by schoolwork. They wish the hard subjects like mathematics or physics would be available in pills. Then they would not need to study them; they could just open their mouths and throw them in. Today, we do not need to do calculation; a calculator can do that for us. Similarly much physical and mental labor can be replaced by machines. But even with the help of technology, we are not advanced enough in the truth of the knowledge of life.

Are you hesitating to become Heaven? Do you not trust yourself? You can trust yourself to be Heaven. You may not like your brother or sister; you may have resistance to what I say. If you cannot believe that harmonizing with other people will make you feel wonderful and Heavenly inside, it may be that the people you are trying to harmonize with are people whose habits, spirit or behavior is harmful or negative. Your hesitation is not that you do not wish to become Heaven, but that you do not wish to harmonize with what is not Heavenly. If such people do not grow enough to want Heaven for themselves and the world, and they give you trouble, do not try to argue or fight with them. Just step aside and respect your own Heavenly energy. Heaven is a little farther than some people can reach.

People who do not grow and develop their Heavenly energy are similar in some ways to small children who do not have enough understanding to behave well. This is like being far from Heaven. You might occasionally give a call or a greeting to such people, but let there be some distance. It is not you who made the distance, it is that they have not grown tall enough to raise their heads into Heaven.

Perhaps many people have given you trouble. Perhaps you have difficulty communicating with some people. Many people make you feel uncomfortable when you are around them. Many people make you cautious. Many people make you nervous. Many people make you nauseous. Many people make you wish not to see them anymore. That is all acceptable.

Are you the person making other people feel they have difficulty to talk to you? Are you the person who makes others feel uncomfortable? Are you the person who makes waves all the time? Are you the person who makes others feel nauseous? Are you the person who makes people not want to see you anymore? You need to brighten your dark spots if you have any. No matter where you are, always be with your Heavenly energy manifesting as love, care, help, friendliness, or at least be at peace.

You might ask, how can we express our Heavenly energy under difficulty? You do not need to do anything. You can be an ordinary, common person. You may be unnoticed. Just do not be harmful. If in a situation where you can help, give help. If you cannot, do not force yourself. Help yourself first. Take care of yourself first. Take care of your health, take care of whatever you need, but do not pull other people down, squeeze people, press people or strip people so that you will feel temporarily better.

You would like to give birth to a Heavenly son or daughter. Yes, I hope your daughter or son will be Heaven. How about yourself? Are you Heaven? Only people with Heavenly energy can give another person Heavenly energy. Practically, each person has Heavenly energy, but does each individual express and extend that Heavenly energy? Each person can achieve naturally and spiritually in an almost equal foundation. Some keep the potential for higher achievement locked away, and are unable to bring the achieved goodness out into the world. The truly achieved person is the one who has had many bad experiences, yet, is not affected by those bad experiences. Or, this person comes to a good understanding and learns the lesson of the experience and then faces the next day fresh and new. He goes on living his purity, remaining with his Heavenly energy well kept and intact. He is an achieved one.

Who are the unachieved ones? They are the people who try to put themselves above Heaven. They do not like to reach out with Heavenly energy of helpfulness and goodness. They like to use their worldly experience to harm other individuals. Were they not Heavenly born just like everybody with an achieved one inside? Their father, mother and ancestors may be nice people. However, their unheavenly energy has increased until they cannot see the world as it is. Those individuals are responsible for their own perception about the world. They wish to reform the world according to how they would like it, like an ant world or bee world. They deny the spiritual growth which we derived from a long time of spiritual evolution. Heaven can be found in very inconspicuous places.

If you are a religious person, you might pray that somebody will come to help you or come to deliver your soul. Would you like to help yourself deliver your own soul? Why wait for a savior to come save your soul? Would you allow poisonous worms, poisonous snakes or fire to keep burning you until you are in a hopeless situation? You can decide before a situation becomes hopeless to make a change. You will know that religion is like a carrot on a stick. Real help is here now when you help yourself. The savior has appeared in your life; no need to wait so long. You can be the messiah for your own life.

One way to help yourself is to learn to be calm. The Heavenly Way teaches calmness. Have you learned being calm? Calm down. Calm down. Once you calm down, your perception will change. The true magic in life is the normalcy of everyday life, peaceful emotion and following the normal routine of life. Calmness, peacefulness and normalcy bring the good result of stability into your life. Stability opens up the way of Heaven.

The problem is not that the people of the world do not do well enough intellectually; the problem is that even though they do well intellectually, the world is still troublesome. There is more killing, more violence and more trouble. This will continue unless you release your Heavenly energy to help the situation. This is why all great sages request that all people extend their Heavenly energy to come forth to realize Heaven in their own lives and in the world.

I do believe people can make advanced weapons and manage those weapons with the potential to kill the entire world in a few seconds. The world needs your Heavenly energy so that all people can live a good life without that fear or killing. Can you do that? Yes, you can, because you are powerful. The power of worship is not the power to smash the world. The power of worship is the power that a person can use to turn himself around from hell-creating, consciously or unconsciously, to being able to extend one's Heavenly energy to others instead. The power you need to do this is found in turning away from the narrow purpose of self-interest, and using your intellectual energy in the correct direction to promote the well being of your personal life and the life of the world.

We do not need more killing weapons. The world does not need to make the government be a strong machine that controls people to make them, in some way, slaves to a big machine. Please help yourself by moving away from causing trouble for other people. When you stop making trouble, you do not need a savior or messiah, because you are already saved.

You are the Heavenly way. The Heavenly way is not a book; the Heavenly way is not in my speech; the Heavenly way is in your heart. My message could be the ignition for you to start extending your Heavenly energy and also to make it grow stronger. If you trust my writing and my speech, the power of your belief can help your life.

If you are stingy and do not like to endow your Heavenly power or Heavenly energy on yourself and the world, there is no way to enjoy spiritual benefit. I am telling you that all of you have a worldly mission. Your mission is no different from mine; it is to bring a better world to all of us. We like to enjoy a healthy world; a healthy world is called Heaven. Have you seen that, can you imagine it? You can imagine many things, why can you not imagine such a simple thing?

You do many things; by what you are doing, you increase the health of the world or destroy the health of the world. Each moment, as we watch what we are doing, we can clearly see whether we are increasing the world's health. We watch how well we perform our jobs. We watch our motives and intentions in our actions. We watch to see that we are not trying to play the hero, but just perform one action after another, in a clear, positive way.

You are Heaven. The world needs your help. We cannot expect anybody besides ourselves to make the world different. Not by political system, not by intellectual system; only when you express your Heavenly energy can the Heavenly health can be realized in the world.

Not Christianity, not Islam, not Buddhism, not Taoism, not any of the sages say it, but you are the sage. In a practical way you are the messiah, the savior of the world. Can you help? Please do it. Do not wait. We cannot wait. There is no more time. During the last 3,000 years, many people have wished to declare themselves as sages who were helping people and the world. So many different religions have been created; this is confusing for many people. So much establishment, so much discrimination, and so much separation has been made conceptually in the world. Can you help do away with all the conceptual confrontation, but safely keep the simple human spiritual customs that we enjoy as the lubrication of our everyday life? Please do it. You are Heaven.

When you meet a friend who has a different religious background, what do you communicate? Usually you extend your Heavenly energy and accept the differences between you. When you reach out your hand to hold the hand of a person of a different background, you are Heaven. Heaven is not just attending a service or mass in your own small church or temple. Religion can be hell if negatively expressed, or if used as a weapon for aggression or fighting.

There is no Heaven unless you are it. There is no hell unless you are it. There is no Heavenly Way unless you become it. There is no messiah, Heavenly kingdom, or god; nothing except what you are.

During this past 3,000 years, have we made much progress, or have we made trouble for ourselves? Let us do away with our troubles by solving them and enjoying the good result of our spiritual awakening, the good achievement we have brought about. We can achieve more.

Science fiction is based on the general human pattern of love and war. What greater expectation, hope or imagination can be extended for the human world, besides love and war? Can there be a third possibility? Yes, Heaven.

There are ambitious individuals who use the existing conceptual inventions to collect people into groups and use them as tools for personal ambition, to control a bigger society. Is China not an example of this?

In these 3,000 years of Chinese history, many monarchs and dynasties have been established by the bitter hand of military victory. And with the same reason, military victory, regimes, dynasties and monarchies have fallen apart and new regimes have arisen. This has been repeated and repeated through generations. Has it truly brought any benefit or good life to people? Military dictatorship can be ended by adopting the achievement of Western society, a genuine democratic system. In that way people can do away with endless physically violent competition for leadership.

War was adopted as a short cut to solve a problem or contention. However, it only builds new problems and new contentions. Thus, no leader needs to push people to run into that dead-end alley over and over again.

This is on a big, worldly scale. Let us return to the importance of our own lives. We come back to focus on our own individual lives, our families, our friendships, work situations and opportunities. It seems in life that enjoyment does not last long, but struggle continues indefinitely. How can we end the struggle? It is simple. When we drive out on the highway or freeway, to the market or anyplace, rather than expecting the world to change, we need to be the ones who first change ourselves. If we change ourselves, the hope for a better world is there. If we do not change, the world will not change, and Heavenly energy cannot be expressed. Only when people come back to their senses and attain higher, clearer understanding will the change towards Heavenly energy happen.

I will close now by saying that in this tradition there is no pushing, no demanding, no asking and no knocking on your door. Without any artificial conceptual embarrassment, we shall embrace as friends. We shall meet each other as common people, as everyday people. We smile at each other, laugh together, enjoy together, and live as good neighbors to make the true Heaven happen in our everyday lives. It can be everyday, as a commonplace occurrence, and it can happen everywhere.

What is the light? Being able to see things. What is spiritual light? Being able to see situations and matters clearly and knowing what you need to do. Some people try to save the world, but they are still in trouble themselves.

They have not yet grown their clear vision or spiritual light. The world cannot wait any longer for its recovery, rejuvenation and health. You decide, you are the one to answer the call, you are the messiah. You can save the world if you develop your spiritual light.

Spiritually, whatever work a person does, it is unvirtuous to use people only as one's stepping stones to reach good fortune, as in the example of evil world leaders. Using others is not the same as depending on your own good work to reach your good fortune. Your own spiritual improvement is your stepping stone to Heaven.

If people who have reached good fortune look back, they wonder how they could have gone through all the difficult experiences. They were naive and young and did not know enough to be scared. They could have run into many troubles, traps and failures. They do not even know how they were able to walk away from all the dangers and troubles they met during that time. They may not have realized that the pure and fearless mind is the fundamental power of each individual plus the virtue of prudence.

Eventually Chinese communism must fall, because the leaders have not had that virtue and spiritual growth. They have not even slight spiritual knowledge, thus they have led themselves into the worst struggle between themselves and the Chinese people and brought only a harsh life to all. They have pulled people away from the Heavenly Way of life to an existence where people must starve. It is a society ruled by soldiers.

Without spiritual improvement, a government is evil. Without spiritual improvement, people are prejudiced. Without spiritual improvement, healers are ineffective. Without spiritual improvement, the world cannot make real progress towards happiness and peace.

Chapter 3

Being Spiritual is not an Attitude

Our spiritual work at this time is to study and review what has been achieved by our ancestors[1]. Although we have progressed to a different stage of development since spiritual knowledge was first initiated several thousand years ago, I think it would be valuable to review the work and discoveries made by all of our human ancestors.

I am talking about the human ancestors of all places. We can consider anyone born before us an ancestor. According to the facts of incarnation and reincarnation, a person could come back to the same family, race and society, but it is possible that in a person's last life or next life, he or she will be born into a different region or race. Spiritually, there is no discrimination of race, nationality, gender or social class.

Today, many people recognize that it is a natural phenomenon for spirits to incarnate into a different time or place. However, reincarnation was not somebody's creation. It is a natural process. Whether you are happy or unhappy about it, it is natural. There is no special privilege handed out by somebody in the Heavenly realm; all human lives and souls are offspring of nature, so all go through the process of reincarnation. Or if you like, we might say that all human souls are the offspring of Heaven.

When you enter human life, you are still sons and daughters of Heaven. This spiritual teaching is often mentioned in the Taoist tradition. We divide the periods before and after a person's birth into two stages called Pre-Heaven and After-Heaven. In the Pre-Heaven stage, before you formed your life, you were a natural spirit; you knew everything. You could not be distinguished as an external object or a person. There was no visual difference because all was oneness. There was no discrimination or difference between

---

[1]Please read my recent work, *Essence of Universal Spirituality* for a review of our ancestor's spiritual practices.

you and what was not you, no separation or boundary that could be marked.

Once you enter the form of a body, then you become a male or female, an Eastern or Western person, and you live in a certain society and have a certain social status. You experience all kinds of discrimination, especially from people who believe that social status, race, gender, etc., are important differences among people. A person who has a natural perspective or background, however, makes less discrimination or classification; to him everything is close to nature.

There is such a big difference between the Pre-Heaven stage of life and the After-Heaven stage. The bondage of the After-Heaven stage is so much and so different from the original stage of life that each of us tries to come back to nature however we can. All individuals and all generations reach out for spiritual achievement to reach the reality of what we originally were.

So, to achieve the knowledge and capability of the Pre-Heaven stage, we first need to know that we are children of nature. The formation of life is a natural process; it does not come to us or stay away from us depending on whether we like it or not. The human soul totally connects with the energy of the sun. The human mind and intelligence are much affected by the moon. The human body and the physical sphere are much affected by the stars.

In the first stage of our lives, we are nature. We have not attained any spiritual awareness and we have not made any spiritual achievement. When we have made spiritual achievement and are highly evolved spiritually, at that time you may be able to attain the self-mastery to enjoy the freedom of entering or leaving a body as easily as people dress and undress themselves. Most people cannot manage, decide or control their life and death. They are totally at the demand, control and management of nature or subject to the conditions present from their birth or the limits of their knowledge about life.

In the initial stage of human life, people still blindly follow the natural cycles and flow of life because they have not yet attained spiritual achievement. Although people might be able to overcome external pressure, often they cannot tolerate the internal pressure of drives, emotions or needs. For example, when a person is hungry, he must eat. If he does not eat, he must die. That is the natural obligation of life. How about sexual disturbance? Can a person feel the disturbance or physiological pressure from that part of his nature and not do anything to act on it? Most people cannot achieve the ability to control their desire or impulses. If they do suppress their desires, most people just wish to please some spiritual giant or monster of their own imagination. However, the spiritual monster is the person himself, nobody else. One's internal sexual pressure is much stronger than any imaginary external spiritual monster a person sets up.

If a person can control the pressure and handle his desires, this is admirable; but he cannot say he has achieved self-mastery until being able to enter and leave life as easily as dressing and undressing himself. Are there actually people who can achieve that? Yes, there are many. However, the cycle of reincarnation cannot be stopped through using religious faith, no matter how hard one tries.

So we know that reincarnation is routine and customary. But religions that try to do something about reincarnation do not actually help. It is not clear what they are trying to do. If you believe in reincarnation, that the soul of a person goes from one lifetime to the next, let us talk, then about the liberation of the soul. Most religions teach about reincarnation of the soul, but some do not touch the subject when dealing with the general public. After reincarnation is taught, the religions also teach about liberating the soul from always reincarnating in a low position to a better state of existence. They teach the theory of karma, which means that if a person does bad things in one life, then bad things will happen to him in the next life. And if a person does good things in this life, then good things will happen to him in the next life. Let us say that there is a person who directly kills human lives, eats mostly meat, has many unhealthy sexual relationships in his life and may have much behavior which is morally unfit. You can say that he does not attain the necessary spiritual evolution to be a decent human person. Religious people may come to him and comment about the theory of karma. They might tell him that it was his bad karma that made him into a beast. Then they might teach him in a religious way to sacrifice all his pleasure and desire in this life to attain a better life for the next time. He is told he can have a good life then.

Some people say, "All the trouble I have! Now I have become like a slave. I suffer difficulty in my life; it is the accumulation of my bad karma, so here I am in this mess. To make things better, I need to follow this spiritual religious practice to eliminate my karma. I need to see what good karma I can gather for my next life." So then a person goes about trying to dissolve his bad karma.

What is a good life? To most people, a good life means lots of money, lots of material provision and wealth, lots of sex and lots of food. The religion teaches people that to improve their karma they should give up sex, money, luxuries and rich food in the hopes of having a good next life. Does this make sense? This is spiritual undevelopment. This teaches a person who already has a "good blessed life" to give up the things that constitute a "good blessed life" to get a "good life." Usually in such a case, the result is that he just saves those desires for the next life. The karma theory cannot be used this way. Primarily, the karma theory is used by religion as a psychological tool to make the followers feel better about what they cannot attain in this life. Is it logical that they would try to suppress or give up their desires in this life so that they can be manifested in the next life, and call that better?

Q: I would say that a better life would be a more peaceful life, not a life of rushing around to grasp many things for oneself.

Master Ni: Right. A peaceful life is spiritual development attained by one's own subjective effort. It is different and more truthful than the religious theory of karma. A peaceful life is what we promote in the tradition of Tao.

However, the conception that most people have of a good life is not of a better, more peaceful life. Why? Practically, it is because many people are desperate in their life situation for more things, more status, more attention, etc. We wish for everybody in the world to have what they need for their healthy survival, but many people go far beyond that and wish to have much more than they need, or they harm other people to get what they desire. This is why we teach people to be natural and accept what they can obtain materially in a good life of hard work, rather than using immoral means to obtain things.

So when somebody promotes a religious faith, if he says "I guarantee that in your next life you will have a better situation," that person usually means more material benefit rather than a peaceful life. In a peaceful life, you might give up whatever material reward is there, because the peaceful life itself is the reward. When you become less desirous, you are no longer excessive in doing things; the reward is to live a balanced healthy life.

If a religion tells you that you are doing something for the afterlife or the next life, you must know that it is a way to attract people to follow them; it is not a spiritual achievement. Truthfully, the way to improve one's next life is to improve one's current life. (It is like a two-in-one bonus.) I am not talking about material improvement, I am talking about spiritual improvement. Spiritual improvement means being able to recognize the difference between right and wrong, having the strength to turn away from doing wrong and turning one's life in the direction of doing right. It also means learning to improve one's own self by improving the mind through good learning, improving the body through good exercise and diet, and improving the spirit through different spiritual practices. It is all done mostly by changing one's habits.

Each moment we are on the path of spiritual evolution to improve ourselves better and better for now, not waiting until the next life. There is a fundamental standard of a natural healthy life. From that, a person builds his spiritual achievement. If he overdoes things, like too much food, too much sex, too much talking, too many possessions, etc., or if he does the opposite which is to give up all the necessities and normalcy of a natural life, what can be called a better life? In the teaching of Tao, we value the balance between the two extremes.

Let us give an illustration: the practitioners of Jainism are ones who see the danger of too much sex, possessions, etc. and try to live their lives oppositely of that. They wear chains around their necks as a symbol of self-restraint and add one more link to the chain each year. They cease many life activities. Others think that a person can be a slave to desire for comfort, so they deny themselves the comfort of a mattress and instead sleep on a bed of nails and add one more nail each year. They give up all the normalcy of life to go to the other extreme which is asceticism, or total denial of material things and desires. They believe their spiritual practice will reduce their karma in order to liberate the soul. But we know that reincarnation cannot be dissolved; it is natural.

It is not only now and only we who deny those practices of asceticism. Around 2,500 years ago Sakyamuni (Buddha) denied those practices. He had tried them himself to see if they were helpful in living a more peaceful life, and when he discovered that they were not, he stopped them and began to teach something different. But now, we need to go even further than the wise Buddha's teachings, because although he made an improvement by denying those practices, his improvement and reflection were for the practices and people of his time. Although he was successful in reducing the numbers of people hurting themselves or dying from un-healthy abuse of their own bodies by not eating, etc., we believe that we need to continue working to improve the modern spiritual view of life.

Now, 2,500 years after Buddha's life, let us review what has happened to his teaching. Buddhists cannot change their basic teaching which devalues the normalcy of life. The original Buddhist teaching urged people to give up a normal life, and live a negative, unproductive life by accepting that worldly life gives one pain and that only by dissolving the worldly pattern of life can a person have no pain. Thus they can rise above worldly trouble. Buddha himself had become ascetic to try to find out how to deal with the pain and difficulty of life. He discovered that it did not work, just as excessive material enjoyment does not work either. So he taught the modified ascetic way adapted from Jainism.

However, after his death, some teachers developed his teaching to be Mahayana or the big school. It is a compromise with worldly life. This life style was retained by practitioners of the monks and nuns of Buddhism. The main attitude towards life is taught to the followers of the big vehicle of Buddhism. Is that the truth that everybody should follow? Is that kind of path natural and healthy?

I would like to tell you a secret that the Taoists know. It is a spiritual teaching so simple that few people believe it, because people like things to be so complicated. It is that anybody who lives a normal life lives a good life. Anybody who works on improving his mind, does not overly think about the problems of his life, maintains well the health of his life substance, has high wisdom.

High wisdom is contained in the normalcy of a good, healthy life. Can you see that? This is why the traditional Taoist books say: Fish cannot depart from water, and life cannot depart from its normalcy. What will happen if fish depart from water? What will happen if a life deviates from the normal path and calls it a spiritual path? Is that type of false spiritual life normal, or worthy to establish? Is it more valuable than the normalcy of life?

It is necessary for spiritual people to have kind hearts and balanced mind from their development. It is unnecessary to view life as bitter, painful and not worthy. It depends on the individual's spiritual development to know what is right.

Can people achieve the dissolution of their emotional pain? Can people resolve their emotional entanglements? They can, more and more, as they grow spiritually. Growing spiritually is a process that happens little by little. It is continual growth and self-improvement.

By the way, one part of spiritual self-improvement is earning an honest living. Not until a person has fulfilled the ability to consistently earn the basic needs of life can that person really consider onself to be on a spiritual path. Then, spiritually, this person can learn more and more.

To earn an honest living is a natural obligation. Doing decent work is one of the best ways to maintain a normal life. Your life energy is a gift from nature to be used in doing positive work for the world, whether noble or humble. Once a person can achieve self-support, his spiritual growth and learning becomes more interesting and has a certain depth or richness to it. There are some great or high achievements that can be attained as one improves more and more spiritually. This comes with many years of spiritual learning.

The correct spiritual way of all people can be described as this: for the fulfillment of natural life, first we need to confirm the necessity and value of the basics, the fundamentals of a healthy, normal life. Anybody who lives in the world can fulfill his natural obligation and provide the necessary sustenance for life. However, such a basic fulfillment will not occur if a person extends his ambition and aggression towards the bread of another person's mouth. Religions that deny the fulfillment of normalcy of the demand of life are not correct. All good life, all achieved life, confirms the basic pattern of life. From there, then look for spiritual achievement and learning. The basic fulfillment comes first.

Second, human people have spirits and can develop them and their individual souls. Spirits are children of nature. But not all spirits or human souls will be reincarnated, or reincarnate with a personal sense. Generally speaking, once the soul reincarnates, the sense of the last life is lost. The only true achievement of a life, improving oneself spiritually to have a good personality, can be carried over into the next life. Generally speaking, in one way, the present life is a part of a continual life. In another way, the new life itself can see the achievement from the past life without mentally remembering the details of the past life.

The only possible spiritual achievement is spiritual freedom above a good personality. A person can attain spiritual freedom by self-mastery through a lifetime of cultivation. It may take many lifetimes to achieve it. Self-mastery is necessary in order to become immortal. Only those who have attained freedom above incarnation and reincarnation are immortals. Maybe it takes longer to understand that only those who achieve freedom to go in and out of their bodies can stop reincarnation. Otherwise, reincarnation is nature. It is nothing to be afraid of, and nothing to welcome; it is just nature.

Spiritual growth works towards achieving independence. It does not happen in an organized fashion, but we could talk about steps or levels. The first step is to earn one's own living through honest work. The second step is to improve one's moral condition and do things to benefit the world. The third step is to quiet and control one's being through learning energy practice. The fourth step is to achieve immortality as an angel. The fifth step is to achieve total dissolution of one's self.

So most important, if in this life you achieve the spiritual awareness of yourself, work to intensify your spiritual awareness and to manage your physical energy to transfer to yr spiritual energy; then finally, your spiritual energy will conform to a transpersonal Heaven. The transpersonal Heaven is above a human's sense of a personified god, Buddha or deity. It is a different truth.

The following step is about liberation from karma. Because you have intuition that makes you afraid of doing certain things because you do not like to create any new karma, you follow the suggestions and guidance of the spiritual religious path to deliver yourself. You must know, however, that if bad karma can send you to a bad place next life, and good karma will send you to a better place next life, then whatever life you become, you are still living in a relative world. Any place in a relative world has pain and happiness, gain and loss, so you really do not surpass the pattern of a general life. So having better karma is not true liberation or true delivery.

Liberating your karma does not mean following a new spiritual practice to attain a better life. There is a more profound spiritual teaching not considered by the Church. It is called "Wu Wei." This is the Taoist term that describes the natural achievement. Truthful liberation is wu wei. Wu wei means do nothing to add to your karma, good or bad; living in an absolute level of beingness. Do not live in a dualistic way or relative pattern. Do it now, in this moment; do not wait until the next life. Liberation and delivery are something you need to do now.

The false understanding of the religious path is based on future reward. However, the truth of balanced living is contained in your natural life now. Here is something else for you to think about: most people are not aware that the world is dualistic; which means it contains opposites such as up, down, in out, man, woman, north, south, etc. Most people think dualistically. One of the goals of spiritual growth is to end thinking dualistically, because dualism tends to create separation between the two opposites rather than creating union between them. Thus, spiritual growth ends the splitting of duality to create an absolute, or unitary, being. Whether you know it or not, you are embodied with the absolute truth of life, and spiritual growth is to help you know that. What else can you call delivery of the soul or liberation of the soul and karma other than knowing your absolute being? The established thoughts of liberation are all in the relative sphere.

A person's soul is the spirit of life. You can bring progress, physically and spiritually to yourself, once you make that your goal of life. I have known many people, who when teenagers, did nothing and knew nothing until they spent several years in the "world classroom." The world classroom is also known as "the school of hard knocks." They do a lot, attain a lot and know a lot after that; it is spiritual growth when they have gained some learning from it and still retain their positive attitude about life.

We also see people who live an ordinary life; they work for the pursuit of their material expansion. Because they never look at the quality of what they themselves bring to the world, they live without growing their spiritual awareness; they never grow at all.

People who grow beyond being able to accomplish their basic needs and reach an awareness of the spiritual level of life understand how important it is to develop their own inner strength.

So, we need to understand that we have a natural obligation to fulfill the physical needs of our lives. It is not until we pass one level that we can go on to the next. People cannot grow suddenly. Ours is the path of internal growing; we do not set up any external discipline on a student. When the student grows up to the level of understanding why it is important to discipline oneself, the student will naturally stop doing the things he or she previously enjoyed that were not helpful to a good life.

Achieving oneself spiritually is a great reward of life. We cannot avoid reincarnation or the possible karma. It is our birthright, deepest inner desire and the highest goal of humankind to attain spiritual growth. If we do, we might attain self-mastery of the soul and attain spirisual freedom in this life time.

Basically, we are individualized persons. Because we have bodies, our spirit also seem to be individualized, but it does not have to always be that way. If we deindividualize our spirit, then we become Heaven again. Only if you have personalized and shaped your life, do all the accompaning negative conditions come about. Once you are highly achieved spiritually, you can deindividualize the sense of life; in that moment, you become Heaven.

In my tradition, we have witnessed that once a spiritual being is highly achieved, at any moment this being can appear in a different form to a person who is spiritually connected. The spiritual being can disappear, then come back. Then he freely vaporizes, then disappears again in the air. Many high spiritual beings can do this and maybe many lower spirits can do it. It is a fundamental achievement. I can hear a noise, a snap; and then suddenly I no longer see him or her. Then, snap; he comes right back in front of me and talks to me, this time as a beautiful woman. Those achievements can be verified from your spiritual learning in this tradition.

However, learning to disappear and reappear differently is not important. It is important to know a little about such things only so that we understand that we are not such limited beings. But it takes growth to go to the advanced stages, so let us review some of the basic, beginning steps. First, attain the means to earn your own living and thus help your physical being. It is your job; it is your life. Second, help your spiritual life by learning more about yourself and improving your mind. It is your job, it is your life. Third, look for higher spiritual achievement to achieve spiritual freedom. It brings independence. It is lots of fun. It is true pleasure.

Chapter 4

Spiritual Self-Realization

1. Spirit Is Not a Single Phenomenon of the Existence of Life

Spirits cannot separate from Chi. The subtle level of Chi is as connected to the spirits as the mind as connected to the body. The mistake of general religions is religious teaching that promotes spirits as a separate existence from physical life. That portrays spirits as groundless.

The ancient ones who achieved in spirit had to achieve in Chi also. For example, Jesus was a fleshly man, though he was highly developed internally. During his a physical life, he was able to extend his energy, his chi, out to perform magic and to help other people. Things he did such as turning water to wine, healing people, casting out demons, walking on water, and multiplying loaves and fishes to feed a multitude are all on the level of energy or Chi. The disciples of Jesus did not understand that this was all done by his internal development. The disciples and the other people knew that he was a special person, but they only saw the external events in his life because the level of spirit cannot be seen with ordinary eyes. As Jesus began to teach and work in the world, he got in trouble by attacking the religious leading class, the Pharisees, and was therefore put to death. After his death, his disciples and other followers wished to achieve what he had achieved internally and tried to create a systematic way to do it, a religion. However, they based their religion on the external events of his life rather than on the internal truth which Jesus had wished to teach.

The majority of his followers did not achieve and attain the chi, only Jesus himself. Today, in many parts of the world, Christianity is only an intellectual or emotional faith. No personal spiritual cultivation and attainment of Chi takes place through the religious rituals.

Jesus mentioned many times that one needs to have faith in oneself, but he did not mention what part of oneself. In his teachings, he described spiritual reality by using terms of family members, such as father and son. To him, the father was the source of his spiritual energy. The spiritual nature of the universe, this source of his spiritual energy, is shared with everybody who knows how to attain the spiritual truth.

Jesus made a good example of both spiritual energy and spiritual truth, for he used his personal achievement in Chi to help other people. For reasons of virtue and righteousness, he did not refuse to give his life to serve the teaching. To him, the universal spiritual source was the Father. This universal spiritual source is the true source of everybody.

Later, people made his teaching into social programs to control other people. I am mostly talking about the Dark Ages, during the time of the Crusades and the Inquisition when government and religion were closely aligned. That type of controlling activity is the opposite of what Jesus taught. Jesus inspired people. His teaching encouraged people to grow naturally. He made many good suggestions but never gave a commandment to people by himself. He never said that only by his name you should pray, and all other names be rejected in prayers. It was the church promotion which restructured his teaching. He talked about the spiritual faith that everybody needs to have. His teaching is simple and easily understood. He was a Taoist who valued the spiritual source.

2. It Is Necessary for Us to Attain Growth from Conventional Faith

In the world, there are two types of spiritual convention. One is to have a faith and let it dominate your life. People put their life energy into it, but the faith is nothing more than a projection of their desires as personal energy projection. If the faith is narrow, then their spiritual projection is narrow. If the faith is twisted, then their projection is twisted. Whether it is a conventional faith or something promoted by a fervent leader, usually it lacks the followers' personal examination of its health and spiritual quality. People must learn from life to attain growth. Otherwise, they are pulled out to follow religious creations, tangible or intangible, that may not be truly helpful to their lives.

The second type of spiritual convention is enlightenment. What is enlightenment? It is moving from what is dark and heavy to what is light. It is internal, which means it happens within a person. In darkness, a person cannot see anything. But as this person slowly attains growth and becomes taller and stronger, his vision also becomes strong. Slowly things begin to lighten up. He can see his environment, and then he can see his own enlightenment. If any kind of faith or strong belief is produced from his enlightenment, it is not a faith that somebody creates for him.

Accepting a religious faith is like putting on someone else's shoes. Another person's shoes may not fit right, but some people put them on and try to make their feet grow to fit the shoes. However, maybe your feet are too big. You cannot fit the shoe, so therefore you need to cut part of the flesh off of your feet to fit the shoes. When externally organized religions try to promote a rigid progression of teachings in this way, people struggle. Some people of more intelligence join because they are looking for spiritual truth, but the religions make it so they need to give up their intelligence and intellectual achievement to fit the program. That is not wise.

Rather than following a certain program, your faith in your own spirituality and confidence in life can come from your own spiritual growth at whatever stage you are in. It must not be something externally that commands you. It must be organic, it must be true. It must not be something that makes external demands on you.

There is something that needs to be pointed out. It is not important to have religious belief, but it is important to be open to all natural spiritual inspiration. People have religious faith. They have a preconception of what a holy man is. So if a person has a faith, he might be biased. If a person is naturally inspired, he will not be biased. Today's problem is that there are few people who are naturally inspired, but some people pick up religious prejudice as their faith and reject true wisdom, true knowledge and true enlightenment.

People used to believe that a savior would come to do things for them. It is a type of hero worship found in old society. This type of psychology is fading in modern times as people discover that good things in life come through their own hard work and intelligent living. People also learn that good things in life come from cooperation and harmony with other people and society. Cooperation is the essence of the life of human society. Strong political rulers or religious leaders cannot be the only ones to take responsibility for the world. They need the cooperation of all people.

In spiritual practice, it is everybody's responsibility to improve one's own spiritual condition and to attain spiritual development. It is no longer the time in human history to extend the hope for one messiah who will deliver all people. Your own growth and evolution is the most interesting and rewarding thing that you can do. Each individual needs to live his own life. Each person has his own evolution. Society is also evolving. As history proceeds, spiritual reality keeps changing; nothing can stop it. Therefore, all of us need to be clear and demonstrate personal spiritual achievement in personal and public life through the practice of individual spiritual self-cultivation.

3. People of Tao

A person who is highly developed internally can extend his or her energy out to help other people. Internal development is different from external development. Most people do not understand internal development; they think they know a person by looking at his face or clothing, or looking at the external events of his life. This is how religions and so many of their followers have become distorted; they are looking at the wrong thing. People have based religions upon what they see - the external events of a sage's life - rather than on the internal truth which a person has attained.

Most religions affect people's spiritual vision like colored glasses. People's intellectual or emotional beliefs also affect their spiritual vision. Only through personal spiritual cultivation and attainment of higher energy can people restore their natural vision.

A sage mentions many times to have faith in oneself, but the sage does not mention in what part of oneself one needs to have faith. By saying to have faith in oneself, the sage is referring to the great spiritual source, Tao, the impartial Heaven. Sometimes the words "father" or "mother" are used in different cultures to describe Tao. Tao refers to the source of one's spiritual energy. This source of spiritual energy is enjoyed by everybody who knows how to attain spiritual truth.

I wish the worldly fathers and mothers to be spiritual examples for their children, by living responsibly and attaining their own spiritual development. Parents who live a natural life can help their children's lives.

A natural life is a good example of both spiritual energy and spiritual truth. A person who lives a natural life can use his personal achievement in higher energy to help other people. For virtuous or righteous reasons, such a person gives life energy for the purpose of helping the world.

People who learn Tao are not like other religious people who walk on fire, sleep on nails, or use one muscle to suspend their bodies on hooks from high poles. They are also not like religious people who speak in tongues, or do other unusual things. Such exhibitions are not good examples for correct spiritual development.

Different shapes of spiritual energy all attain certain expressions of power. Hanging from a hook, walking on fire, etc. are all examples of the power which can be produced by strong faith. The spiritual energy generated by a person through desire or intense prayer can bring limited temporary powers or other unusual things such as these.

People of Tao do not promote any conceptual or worldly faith. They are not aggressive. They allow everything to change. They do not encourage people to be winners in the worthless worldly competition. They know that the person who is ambitious to be in control of everything is the one who fails inside. The same thing happens in politics as in religion. Spiritual truth is universal; it is not limited to only one race or one tribe.

You can see that faith, at most, produces the power of fantasy. Instead of fantasy, truthful spiritual energy helps people attain power in life.

Therefore, no special or assertive way can be recommended for people to follow. No one should say one nation or state is for all people. That is against spiritual truth. If anybody were externally strong enough to put the whole world under his personal control, there is still the subtle law of changes that would not allow such control to last. It always happens that if any kind of leadership has strong external control, internal change will occur. If internal change is not allowed, people become sick. Their organic nature will die off.

Some ancient leaders had the ambition to teach one faith or one religion for all people. Because there is competition among different religions, the leaders or the followers often become aggressive. If all people were coerced into becoming followers of one religion, although externally things might look harmonious, internal change bringing discord would occur.

Some strong leaders wish to put a country and all its people under their own unified management. This has also been tested. Before much time passes, a negative result is seen. Any time people are coerced to conform to external sameness, trouble or change happens.

People of Tao do not promote worldly change or attack people at all. They allow everything to be under change. They do that because they know that there is no winner and no loser in the big sphere; everyone is the same.

4. Realize Heaven by Restoring our Kindness from the Deep Universal Spiritual Nature

In our daily lives, our business contacts and all other spheres, sometimes people offend and challenge us, and we get upset. Sometimes, one's hatred becomes strong, which truly brings misfortune into one's life. One way of psychological purification is forgiveness. It is right that everyone needs to try to make great forgiveness work for oneself. One who truly achieves great spirituality can be an example of the virtue of forgiveness.

We might consider using seasonal holidays to have more spiritual significance rather than only following common custom. Holidays can be used for outdoor activities, etc. They also can be used for personal spiritual purification. Let us make them a time for our own spiritual purification. Forgiving is one of the practices.

All people need to try to forgive whatever other people have done to offend them. In one's heart, in one's feeling and in one's mind, if one still holds hatred, one can try to learn from the good example of forgiveness of other people. Only in that way will you bring about your own spiritual growth. When you do so, you have made another step and will achieve higher. Therefore, to spiritually developed people or people of good spiritual understanding, any customary holiday can be a day of spiritual purification and forgiving.

The New Years holiday comes at the end of the year. It is a time to check out your emotion to see if you have hatred inside you. Hatred is a kind of poisonous vapor inside a person which undermines one's health and the balance of one's mentality. So learning forgiveness is important for your life. People do not directly see the benefit for themselves of forgiveness; however, they punish themselves by holding hatred or dislike.

There are many people who appreciate the teaching of Tao. I recommend they still celebrate the holiday of Christmas; although, because their spiritual development is reaching a different stage, they can make Christmas a day of forgiveness rather than just for giving and receiving gifts.

The end of the year is also a time to accept yourself. It is a time to check out your emotion to see if you have a big hatred or small dislike inside of you that makes your internal being imbalanced. Such hatred or dislike makes you unable to accept yourself. It is important for you to accept yourself; from accepting what you are, all good possible improvements can be made. By accepting yourself and forgiving others, you will bring health back to yourself. By forgiving, you make your life lighter and decrease your spiritual burden. When you hate people, you may not even know it, but you punish yourself first. With hatred, you bend down your own spiritual health.

Chapter 5

The Way of Reaching Spiritual Growth

Let us probe some important understandings which connect with our spiritual learning. In ancient times, developed teachers taught their students that there are three spheres of natural energy in cyclical transformation. The three great spheres of being are the different stages of spiritual evolution of each individual being. Nature moves from the lower spheres in the direction of the high sphere, and becomes more essential by changing from the rough structure to the most refined spiritual energy. The force of each forward movement creates the force of pushing away. Thus, in the movement of becoming more essential, something is thrown away or left behind. This is how nature forms its destiny.

There are two great spheres from which the three basic spheres or Heavens of existence are developed: ("Heaven" is used here as a synonym to mean sphere, level or range.)

I. The sphere of the unformed: Natural energy of all levels.

II. The sphere of the formed: All matter, objects and living beings.

In the sphere of the formed, there are three Heavens of beings:

1. The Heaven of form, which includes (1) material which is with form; (2) all life with form; and (3) things like stones and inorganic matter.

2. The Heaven of desire, which includes (1) all life with simple desire of eating and mating, like animals; (2) the life of multiple desire like human people; and (3) lower spirits which have subtle form with certain desires. The above mentioned three types of life all have individuality.

3. The Heaven of non-desire: (1) spirits as the universal natural essence; (2) the return of the spiritual evolution of a lower being; and (3) the high spirits. The above three levels of the Heaven of non-desire are still communicative and responsive. However, individuality dissolves. The highest spirits become the soul of the entirety of nature.

I have given you the outline; now let us enter the discussion. I am emphasizing the spiritual evolution of human life. I would like this teaching to serve as a spiritual direction, not as the establishment of any new or old intellectual knowledge.

The first sphere is 'the Heaven of being,' or 'Heaven of form.' There are lives with form; therefore, there is the Heaven of forms where we are as the formed life, but it exclusively includes things and bodies with forms.

The second level is 'the Heaven of desire and multiple desires,' or 'Heaven of desire' which is a general, low level earthly life. The Heaven of desire may only have two basic kinds of desire: mating and eating. Stones and rocks do not have desire. In human knowledge, anyway, stones and rocks do not have desire, or if they do, we do not describe it that way.

In the second level Heaven, where there is the development of mentality, there are multiple desires. Beings and lives have all kinds of desire, including the desire to know, live forever, enjoy, occupy and be creative, including the pursuit of social glory. This sphere can be simplified to be called the Heaven or level of multiple desires. Or we could call it the Heaven of refined desires, because it holds the possibility of refining those desires to be better and higher energy projections. The desire for creativity and so forth is not the same kind of desire as most people have, of man desiring woman, woman desiring man, a hungry person desiring food, and so forth.

Earthly life begins with mating and eating. Accompanied with mating and eating is competition. Therefore, mating, eating and competition bring fighting. Thus, the basic lower sphere lifestyle includes three things, mating, eating and fighting, but fighting comes from the competition for mating and eating. This means to fight with a competitor, and it also means the fight to get the prey for eating for mating. So at the unrefined level of life, sometimes all the possible opportunities come by means of warring and fighting. The best fighter takes the best opportunity.

This level is limited. Sometimes the impression of life produced on this level is, "Life is fighting. Fight is life. Life is taking. Life is yielding to no one." People start to believe that everything comes from fighting. After the refinement of life comes, cooperation and harmony are also known, valued and recognized, and living beings come to a different sphere. However, this sphere or level still is included in the sphere of desires because any motivation behind the action is a desire. Whatever motivation, realized or unrealized, or how each person behaves, if it is not out of looking for material gain, it must be looking for emotional satisfaction.

If the behavior is not caused by looking for gain or profit, it must come from morality. Morality is the highest motivation, because once you touch something out of morality, it comes to a transition from the sphere of desires to the sphere of non-desires. This pushes the being's life to enter a higher Heaven.

The higher or third Heaven is called 'the Heaven of non-desire.' Although stones and rocks have no desire, they do not have a conscious mind like all lives, so this Heaven does not apply to them. Because the third Heaven is the progression from the second, it is also 'the Heaven of pure rationality.' It is the higher development of the second. It is called the 'Heaven of pure love' or 'Heaven of pure law,' or 'the Heaven of purity.' In this sphere, things are not done, manifested or unmanifested by certain forms or by especially fixed, concrete forms. Nor are things associated with desires, like the ones we have already described in the Heaven of multiple desires. If things are not done by form or desire, how are they done? Things are done by influence. This level is called the Heaven of pure law, Heaven of pure principle or Heaven of rationality.

The ancient developed teachers used the teaching of the three Heavens. When I became a student and a teacher, I produced my reflection of it. I believe its purpose is to show the students that spiritual learning must have three levels of study and achievement. On the first level, you learn something through a formality. This is something that has some form: you learn it and practice it, otherwise it cannot be learned. Then from the learning, from the styles and the forms, you come to a different, higher stage. The second, higher stage is something more subtle, like a simple form. All existing formalities must have a purpose, reason, function, cause and desire behind them. This comes to a different level. When you come to learn the formality of spiritual practice, you just learn it, you do not know it. Then on the second level, you understand the motivation behind it. Are your motivations developed enough? Are your motivations refined enough, or is your motivation still limited to the Heaven of forms? Or have you grown spiritually in the sphere of good understanding to move above the frame of formality? Formality includes the shaped or tangible forms and the conceptual structure. This leads you to reach the third Heaven through the first and the second levels.

The teaching of spirituality is not an easy job. Sometimes the teachings contain social education, social behavior, or personal good habits, including sexual education. A good student knows what level is social education, correct social behavior or what will make him a learned person in the general world. However, some people mistake the level of social education to be higher spiritual education. For example, some people learn tantra as a way to be immortal. If they follow this practice out of desire, then it limits them to the Heaven of desires. Also, if any person has interest in being an immortal, a god, goddess, or a great one and if it happens out of desire, then one's spiritual learning and one's spiritual level are also limited or confined to the Heaven of desires.

By speech, thoughts and actions, each person reflects what he is learning. What he does shows the teaching underlying it. From the level of the lower sphere, the students ascend to a higher level. This level of spiritual teaching that has no formality is a pure teaching. It is a pure path. It is also like a teacher who transmits knowledge directly to your spirit. The teacher's personal achievement of personal spiritual energy can be transmitted to the student. He transmits the highest level of teaching as the pure law, pure principle or Heaven of rationality, directly to the student. When the spiritual student comes to this level, he is no longer attached to formality. He no longer holds any dispute. Now the student is already achieved, because his spiritual learning no longer comes from desire.

There are differences and disputes between the low and the high, and among the differences of all the formalities in spiritual learning. If anything comes out of desire, once the desire is satisfied, the desire has died. Anything can be born or die is not everlasting. If something can be changed, then it is still in the sphere of changeability. Anything in the sphere of changeability has not reached the unchanging subtle truth. Therefore, the highest learning is the subtle truth. The unchanging subtle truth is the very essence of the spirituality of nature, the universe and each individual. If each individual spiritual student comes to this level, no formality or highly motivated desire can disturb or motivate him anymore; he only responds. His spiritual responsiveness just responds with pure law.

Therefore, spiritual teaching was composed on three levels, but to most people's understanding they become three Heavens: the Heaven of forms, the Heaven of desires or refined desires and the Heaven of pure law, pure being or rationality. The spiritual teaching was originated in the form of three levels, but to present it to ordinary people, it was taught as three Heavens.

Q: I wish for the benefit of our listeners that you would define the word desire. I know a spiritual teacher who seems to have lots of desires. For example, wanting to have breakfast. Is that a desire, or something different?

Master Ni: That is a good question. You have a confusion about desire being something issued by mind and something that is a natural instinct without being associated with mentality.

For example, a person eats food. It is a necessity. If a person says, "I like Chinese food, French food, a royal feast or some delicious ice cream for my breakfast," that is a desire because it is a mental extension, beyond necessity.

Q: You talked about starting with the level of form, and the next is the level beyond form. You still have to use the form when you get to the level beyond form, because even the great practitioners of Taoist cultivation still use the form of T'ai Chi Movement to achieve what is beyond the form. If you do not learn the form, then you cannot learn what is beyond it, right?

Master Ni. Right, for the one who achieved in T'ai Chi. Such a person is able to express achievement in that form or no form. The higher the achievement, the less the formality is seen in fighting. The high goal is to transfer the achievement of T'ai Chi practice to one's everyday, practical life, in being able to dissolve friction or conflict with others without any form. It means there is no need to see the policeman or go to court, or even to carry on an argument. This is the correct understanding.

It means practically, do not be attached to a certain form. Forms are to attain freedom, not to restrain your movement. Most students learn things and become attached to one form, but the best form is freedom. Sometimes we talk about two levels, the formed and unformed, or the formed and the formless. In talking about the spiritual level, sometimes we cannot use the words unformed or formless. The reality of highly spiritually achieved ones can be formed as they wish. The general conception of form cannot apply to or limit their freedom. They take any form.

For example, when we study the teaching of Chuang Tzu, we read that a piece of natural energy, like a piece of water energy, can change to be a fish. The fish can change to be a bird. The bird can change to be a human being. The human being can change to be anything. Most people admire paintings or statues of divinities with auras at their heads. They respect those forms. They do not see that the high spiritual beings can take any form without losing their divinity. A high divine being can approach you with any form and sit with you, but still not lose its divinity.

This is hard to talk about because words and language are limited. Spiritual reality is not limited, but trying to talk about it is difficult. Being on the level of the unformed or the formless can never truly describe spiritual achievement or spiritual reality, which has no limitation. Thus, the goal of all the teaching is for the student learn the language, and finally go beyond the language to learn truth.

Now, I come back. Those three divisions, or three Heavens, were beliefs that were held firmly by many students for around 2,000 to 3,000 years. Many spiritual teachers talk about the three Heavens, and of course none of the spiritual students think they like to live in the Heaven of the formed. Neither do they think they like the Heaven of refined motivations. All the students think, "I'm going to achieve the highest! - the Heaven of the pure subtle law. At that time, nothing can attack or bother me. At that time, I will have true freedom." However, when you teach a big group or the masses of people, you have to have some formed, fixed theories or principles, or else people will not understand anything. The truly achieved ones and the learned students can see through the formality for its truthful meaning.

Whether an existence is complicated or simple, the three spheres can never be singly established, nor can they be separated into components of form, energy and reason. They are always integrated as any simple or complicated existence. Therefore, highly achieved spiritual students or teachers know the Heavens are a formality of theory to teach the secondary level of students until they can go beyond the language. Some lower teachings never make it beyond the language, yet they still teach the formality of theory. This is why the Integral Way is the highest, most complete teaching available; it has gone beyond the formality. It helps people move from a low stage to higher and higher stages of spiritual learning and truth, yet they still value the fundamentals of a balanced worldly life.

Once students are achieved in spiritual learning, they know that wherever and whenever, "I am being." Someone who is not achieved might ask, Being what? Being where? It is purely a matter of the "I" that enjoys the beingness or the non-beingness, the formed or the unformed. The limitation of achievement can be caused by the difference of levels. It is not the division of the Heaven of the formed, Heaven of refined motivation, Heaven of pure law or separateness. It is oneness. At the beginning of one's spiritual learning, because of the discrimination from the analytic mind (the conceptual habit), you go through the process of adjusting your level to meet the level of study. But you will not continue to use the same process because you have reached the correct understanding and level of teaching.

General religious followers are sort of like religious cattle. Religious cattle have no way of talking about spiritual development. However, the process of lower learning should not be a reason for a person's lack of spiritual growth. A person can go beyond the obstructions of the religious or social processing he or she has been through. Going beyond one's old learning is the process of discovering truth, step by step.

This is just the beginning. It is an introduction to carry the mind and soul to a new range. Now I will talk about a different way of spiritual teaching.

Q: My question has to do with formed and not formed. You spoke about not getting attached to any one form. I think you mean external form like a statue or something like that.

Master Ni: No, attached to your own human being form.

Q: How do you do that? Let me tell you my experience. When I start a new job, I go into the job and am totally unrefined in relation to the new people, new tasks, etc. After I have been there a while, I have learned the external form of the job, such as what goes where, and how to do it. And if I keep working there longer, eventually, because most things repeat themselves, I go beyond that level and get onto more of an energy level. I become mentally and energetically faster than the events around me, become refined and very good at my job. The refinement makes things go smoothly in my day and my life, and it takes me to a higher vibration of being, and my spiritual energy grows.

Yet, every time I go to a new job, it seems that I have to start out unrefined again, and start out learning all over again. The refinement seems to vanish for a long time, and it takes a lot of mental effort to learn a new job, which decreases my spiritual energy.

It seems that my refinement is related only to the form of that job or the outer circumstance in my life. So my question is, how can I be refined without my refinement being in relationship to a form such as a job, an exercise or even my own body?

Master Ni: I will consider that what you say is not a question, it is another good illustration of learning the formality, then you attain the essence, doing different jobs with a fluent energy. Fluent usually describes language, but I would also like to use this word to describe the working energy that does everything smoothly.

You say that if you change to a new job, the new formality is learned and starting is hard. I think it is a matter of stage; if you have different opportunities to learn different things, you finally become totally achieved. There is only one principle in all kinds of jobs. There is only one way, one simple way, one good way for all formalities. Though the formalities are different, the essence is the same. It is: what is the best, most simple way to accomplish the formality?

Let us say a person goes to law school. To be a lawyer, there are numerous books, laws and declarations that need to be learned. Does the student really need to read and remember all those things? No. He or she learns the fundamental things; it is knowing how and where to look in the books for the regulations that makes a person a lawyer. Because there is so much information with regards to a certain aspect of law, if he knows more about it and is more familiar with it, a lawyer can specialize. But the principle behind the work is the same.

That is, a person learns the principle in order to understand the nature of the work. The small details can be fulfilled by one's secretary or assistant. The secretary completes a part of the work without learning the whole picture of the whole job. It is equally true for a medical doctor; even though there are so many small branches of medicine, the basics are the same. There is always a basic principle behind the different jobs.

Spiritual teaching is different from that. I believe God is a metaphor. In general, people or religions think that God must be a glorified being and many people who can see great light from him bow before him. It is, in reality, a misconception. The divine nature of the universe can be any way, can be any form. For example, the Chinese students of Buddhism wish that some day they can sit in the shrine above the altar like Buddha, whose body is gold, eyes closed and smiling. This is why they learn. They do not learn the reality. People go to different churches where they have different promotions and different images. That is a spiritual art, a spiritual skill. It is not the truth beyond the forms.

Once you learn the reality beyond the forms, it is Tao. We talk about the divine nature, the unformed truth and the formless truth: it is Tao. If you attain Tao, you attain everything.

As I say, people learn to be electricians, carpenters or plumbers. There is a fundamental, undescribable essence behind all the handcrafts or manual techniques. Though it is hard to describe, the common training is the same. A person may sell cars, boats, clothes or cosmetics. Although the things being sold are different, there is a certain principle or practice behind being a salesman. I am not talking about advocating that people buy one's goods. A responsible salesperson also checks out what he is going to sell. To learn salesmanship is not necessarily to cheat buyers.

Q: It seems that there are cheaters in every profession, as well as those who bring their good energy.

Master Ni: Right. We have been talking about the good aspects, not about the bad things.

The ancient spiritual teachers were so interesting to observe. It was the level of people that forced them to use the terms Heaven and hell. They had to do something to illustrate good and bad in understandable terms.

However, those who have attained the higher Heavens can read about it to confirm their understanding that indeed there is a reality other than physical reality. If a person tries to talk about it to friends who are ordinary people, they will deny his understanding of the truth, and he may end up thinking himself crazy!

Q: Which teaching?

Master Ni: The teaching of the three Heavens. In Taoism, we always use a cauldron to symbolize the Heaven of form, the Heaven of purpose and the Heaven of pure truth. Those three things cannot be separated.

Also, in the original Chinese society, thousands of years before communism, the ruler or sovereign was the symbol, but the true ruler was people's education. What was their education? Basically, it was self-government, individually, in a small community or big society. When a dispute arose, the people referred to Heavenly law and to conscience. I believe in the Western world you use the word conscience to describe how people are supposed to feel when they have done something wrong. However, most Western people have forgotten how that feels, or are un- aware of any connection between their action and the bad feeling. But for Chinese people, in general, when there is a fight or a dispute, the people refer to conscience and Heav- enly law. Chinese people will say, "By Heavenly law, I never did that, I never said that." Some of them use the words together, "By Heavenly law, my conscience, I never did that, I never attempted to do that." People defend themselves in that way.

The terms "Heavenly law" and "conscience" are two different things, two different conceptions. Heavenly law sounds like something beyond individual existence that expresses justice and fairness, or righteousness. Con- science is one's consciousness of morality, which is some- thing that grows inside a person. The conscience develops when somebody is subtly aware of right or wrong, individu- ally; it is a subtle conscious mind.

Q: I still get stuck on the word "morality."

Master Ni: American morality is different. American morality is the concept taught by religion. What you do not know is that morality also includes ethics. Maybe you prefer to use the word "ethics" which was also discussed by the Greek philosophers. You might like to use the word ethics from now on, to avoid your conceptual obstruction.

The sense of being ethical is something that grows inside; it is human nature from the inside. Later scholars from the beginning of the Sung dynasty, 1000 years ago, said Heavenly law must be studied. Then somebody who had a deeper reflection, said, How do we know Heavenly law? The answer was: Because we have a conscience, we know Heavenly law. Then came a further question: If our conscience grows from inside, from a humanistic tendency, can it grow independently of the Heavenly law? The answer to that question was, Absolutely not. If not, then the division of Heavenly law and conscience is unnecessary.

That was a strong statement made in that time. It was a good ideological discovery that Heavenly law is conscience, and conscience is Heavenly law. The internal truth is the external truth, the external truth or basic truth is internal. There is no difference.

The reality of life is that humans exist in different spheres. Some part of it is on the level that is visible, audible and touchable. There are also the spiritual levels. All spiritual levels, whether you believe in them or not, are all untouchable, inaudible and invisible.

No existence can be without form; all existence has capacity. It is formed. The non-formed natural energy still has its capacity. We will not talk about desire; we will talk about energy. Desire is the transformation of physical and mental energy. Yet, the transformable energy of life still involves a more basic form of energy. There must be energy behind the formed. Even a stone has energy: stone energy has gravity. Whether it be a rough, coarse existence, on a high or low level, important or unimportant, huge or small, significant or transient, all have energy.

The Heaven of the formed and the Heaven of unformed are both the Heaven of energy. As for the Heaven of law, we know that the movement of energy produces a certain pattern. When this pattern is known and becomes controllable, it is a law. A law or pattern cannot be a separated existence. The matter is not beyond the law, and the law is not beyond the matter. For example, the activity of mind has its field. The field transforms its energy to participate in the activity. The Heaven of law cannot exist beyond the Heaven of matter.

The teaching of the Heavenly law is viewed as external existence. Because we live in a sphere, the Heaven or sky enormously envelops us. There is energy movement constantly in the sky and on the surface of earth. With subtle observation, a person can see that there is a Heavenly law that operates in the universe that gives us the stability of the natural environment in which we can live. This harmony behind everything is the Heavenly law which is for all people, good or bad; one who learns the Heavenly law can be happy with what one can be.

Unrefined or bad people are unhappy. They do things from their wish to be in a better position with something, but eventually because they cannot accept what they are, they do not do better, and things stay the same for them. By their undevelopment, they only make a disturbance for their fellow people and themselves.

The recognition of the externally existent Heavenly law is the result of the internal growth of conscience. Conscience is Heavenly law and Heavenly law is conscience; it is one thing. At the same time, desire is energy. Any motivation or any purpose is energy. Without energy, no desire can be extended.

Theoretically, philosophically and in their clarity, the scholars of the Sung Dynasty made progress in saying that there is no division between Heavenly law and conscience. For example, a single Chinese word must have a shape, pronunciation, intonation and meaning. Can the five things be separated? No, they must be one. Let us take another example of a composition. A teacher of Chinese assigns a student to write a composition. From the composition, the teacher can see how much achievement in grammar, rhetoric and writing the student has. Can the writing be separated from the grammar training and the rhetorical skill? It cannot.

It is important for all students to know this. At the beginning, students are confused by the different forms, language and terminology of all the religions. The pointed roof of the Christian church, the round roof of the Islam church, the different terminology each religion uses, are all human creations that serve as metaphors for something beyond our creation. We use this something describable as an attempt to show the indescribable sphere. All the books and all the different religions are on the same level, because each one is a literary attempt to describe, narrate or discuss the indescribable, high truth of spirituality. It does not matter whether an achieved one uses a Bible, the Koran, a Sutra or an African holy book; he knows all of them are metaphors. Some metaphorical descriptions are more skillful than others, some are more complicated and some are simpler. However, they are all on the same level. Nobody can really show spiritual reality, because it is indescribable.

Because of their social backgrounds and customs, it is hard for spiritual students to start to learn spiritual reality. If they are really attached to those backgrounds, they unfortunately usually becomes a reason for saying, "Our way is better, we are right and you are wrong." They never achieve or attain Tao.

I would say that Tao is unreachable by any religion. The levels of different teachings are so different. Though you can take my picture or describe me, the photo or book is not the real me, a thousand years after I die. To some extent, it is a description of me in some part, correct or incorrect, complete or incomplete.

So I have simply made a conclusion: I would wish all good students to learn to reach high spiritual achievement directly and go beyond the disputes about differences among religions. Those religions can be useful. They are good at metaphor, and they make the world so colorful, so interesting, positive and enjoyable for us in the early stages of our growth. But the one of real growth does not embrace that or hold that as truth.

My responsibility in teaching Tao is not to teach religion; however, I am connected with, affected by and related to all religions. Therefore, I discuss them repeatedly.

Q: Could you tell how this relates to the three level of purity, the three San Ching?

Master Ni: The San Ching is a special classification of energy. It is a goal of Taoist achievement. Let me go back to talk about the three spheres.

At the beginning, the ancient wise ones decided the universe had three levels or was a triangular unity. This great triangular unity describes the three spheres. First is the spiritual sphere or Heaven.   Second is the material sphere, or earth, because all matter is similar to earthly nature. In modern terms, we call it physical nature or the physical sphere. The third sphere is that of human life; it is the integration of the other two.   The interrelation or intercourse of spiritual energy with physical energy produces lives.   Human life belongs to that category, therefore Heaven, earth and humans make up the great triangular unity of the universe.

Q: When you talk about physical energy, you are talking about material objects, things.

Master Ni: Right. The earth does not mean just the globe, the earth as a globe, as a planet. It means the entire physical sphere. This is what the ancient wise ones classified as being in the earth category.

The three existing spheres compose the universe.   It was only in a later time that we began to talk about the Heaven of the formed, the Heaven of desire and the Heaven of pure law.   That is another version of the three great triangle unity of the universe, Heaven, earth and people; it is just a different way to talk about it.

We return to the basics: all material things in the physical sphere have forms.   Forms are not necessarily living.   Stones and all other material objects are made of the five elements: wood or vegetation, water, metal, earth and fire. It is the interplay of different energy, formed and unformed that brings life. Practically, life is a higher evolution of energy. When things come to life, if they have instinct or complete desire, they fall into the Heaven of desire. So the first is the Heaven of the formed. The second is the Heaven of desire.

Even if we suppose, like most people, that Heaven is a beautiful place, a paradise with all refined things or wonders, we would put it into the category of the Heaven of the formed. Practically, the Heaven of the formed means all material things. Thus a 'Heavenly paradise' of beautiful things would fall into this category.

The second level, the Heaven of desires, practically means that humans and other living creatures all have desire. You ask, why does a sage have desire for breakfast? He is a sage, but he is alive. All living creatures, no matter what their level, very earth-bound or highly achieved, have desire and instinct to eat. Your hunger will tell you. If a person has hunger that tells him to eat, or even if he fasts for forty-five days in a box at the bottom of the ocean and achieves special skill in preservation of life energy, he still needs to eat and breathe when he comes out, so he is still in that category of having desire. It does not matter who you are.

Then, there is the Heaven of the formless. It is no non-existence; it is existence, but with no form or with no fixed form. It can form itself as it wishes.

So the three Heavens or spheres are: first, the material sphere or the range of material; second, human sphere and any life with desire to eat and mate; and third, the highest, spiritual sphere, where there is no form. So there is the formed level or category, life with desires, and formless beings.

Because modern people only recognize the formed level of existence and the desire level, they cut off their heads. They do not know the level of the unformed.

In this discussion, the most important point is: "Our ancestors, by their development, could see the level of the formed and the life with desires; also, they verified a level of unformed or formless life." But the formless life is now neglected by modern people.

The ancient spiritual people proved that the evolution of the entire universe is from the low sphere to the high sphere. First there is the formed material which evolves to be the life with desires. From the life of desires there is much restraint, inconvenience and obstruction, all at this level of being.

Let us talk about being. It has three spheres, too. The first, which is not high, is formed. It takes many millions of light years for the formed sphere of being to develop into the life of desires. If, however, the life of desires attains self-consciousness or spiritual self-awareness, then there is a possibility for that person to achieve another, higher level of absolute freedom. That level also has different divisions; I will talk about that later. Now I need, first, to give you a basic understanding.

The second level of being is not the level of high being. It is the level of the result of one great leap of evolution and it is characterized by having desire.

The third level of being is the level of high being. The essence of high being is formless, thought it can take any forms.

We come back to say that all three levels are Chi or energy. The three levels of being - formed with no desires, formed with desires and formless - are basically energy.

Now we come to the spiritual goal in our tradition expressed by the wise ones. They put three names on those levels: Tai Ching, Sang Ching and Yu Ching. The level of Tai Ching can be achieved in worldly life by refining oneself. Tai Ching pertains to the fact that once we have a human life, we have all kinds of desire and all kinds of need for material support. But from that foundation, we can still move upward and achieve ourselves to attain the higher energy. So a person who lives with the energy of spiritual gentleness and clarity is a sage; he must have a pure life. His desire is not so strong.

If it is a man and he sees a beautiful woman, the sage has desire. His desire might be to look at her, feel pleased and have a good feeling. But that desire would be limited to experiencing a good feeling and enjoying the beauty, but not acting on the desire, saying "I am going to seize, take or contaminate the object of my desire." The same thing is true of other things, for example, a high position or great amassment of valuable treasure. Most people will go for what is valuable. The achieved one, however, gradually decreases the strength of desire. He still has desire, but the strength of that desire does not bind him any more. Whether he does something or not, either way is okay. If he does it, surely it may be from desire, but he can immediately see with his spiritual achievement whether it will cause trouble, be inconvenient, damage his health, damage his harmony of life and so forth. Then he just restrains himself from the action if it is unwise. He just forgets it, that is all. All of this relates to the Tai Ching level.

The level of Sang Ching is that of a spiritual person who is achieved. He can make the unformed spiritual world communicative and come to assist his worldly mission or worldly goal. In ancient times, most people lived a life based on agriculture; water and rain were important. Some achieved masters can reach the water energy through spiritual methods. For example, in the case of a drought, the water deities in nature would help by immediately causing rain. The experienced masters would only ask for three or five inches of rain and manage things well from the beginning. If an inexperienced student asked for rain, when the rain energy came, without giving any limit, maybe it would cause a downpour when the rain energy came, and they would get too much!

Q: Is that also the kind of natural situation where you are attempting to do something in your life that seems really impossible. It seems that there is no way that thing could be accomplished, so perhaps you give up struggling. Then, all of a sudden, you notice that things just seem to come into place by themselves and everything works itself out beautifully for all concerned?

Master Ni: It is a little different. You see, in the Tai Ching level, you are already not struggling, but you work, you live a real life; you are not escaping anything.

We have already described Tai Ching or primal purity. Tai Ching is practically an achievement of the highest internal harmony and the great harmony with nature, all without losing personal wholeness or integrity. It generates the natural harmony of giving birth to life. It is not breaking or smashing, but spiritual harmonization with the great subtle law. If you agree with the subtle law, you are one with everything: that is Tai Ching.

The other level, Sang Ching, pertains to maintaining your spiritual power. By the spiritual practice you achieve, you really prove the spiritual world. It is like every day you take care of your daily life, internal spiritually, external spiritually and the entire world spiritually. It is just like looking at a finger, as clear as that. You not only look at the finger, but you can control it. That is possible. I learned those high secrets, but it is forbidden by Heaven to teach them; only if a student is ready can he be taught. If a person is not ready, he can go mad or crazy; learning a little bit is useless. It takes many years, many lifetimes to evolve to a stage where one can learn those things. A teacher cannot be fooled about a person's stage; usually people have ambition and try. A true spiritual teacher cannot be bribed, either. Only the teacher can see whether it would be harmful to teach someone and of no use. This is why we tell people to make themselves ready in personal virtue. Virtue means personal character. Most people cannot join.

I wonder how many in history were achieved in each generation. They are all immortals. They do not like to interfere with the growth of the general human mass, but at the request of the existing achieved people in the world, they help so that the world can start to turn around. The high beings can be reached by the people of the world;, otherwise they do not like to bother human people. What humans enjoy, such as glory, pride or prosperity, is a cyclic matter. The lives of the high beings are already beyond the pattern of cyclic human life. Their lives are not lived in the yin/yang pattern any more.

I would like to utilize one word to describe the Sang Ching level. It is the high potency of nature. Why use the word potency? It is not enough to express the pure power. It is not the general conception of power; once you are involved with power, there is struggling and competition. But there is something higher than that. Power becomes an ambition, a poison to your spiritual reality. I would describe Sang Ching as the subtle potency or clarity which is unsurpassable. It can turn the world around, turn an individual life around and turn one's environment around. At the least, a person can turn himself around without putting himself in a drowning or struggling situation, positively give help and amass good influence.

Sang Ching is the supreme purity. It is the level of spiritual power performance which guides, governs and adjusts nature. It reshapes nature and assists life.

The Yu Ching level is the level of transparent purity, which is the power of supervision. It is the wisdom of the sages. It produces the clarity of guidance. It also produces clarity in fulfillment.

So, Tai Ching is the power of peace. Sang Ching is the power of practice, and Yu Ching is the power of guidance. They are totally united. At the highest level of universal energy, Tai Ching gives birth but does not own, Sang Ching furthers life but does not lord over it, and Yu Ching guides the life but does not take credit for it. All are one divine nature which reaches those who nurture a similar energy within themselves. These are the three important measurements of divinity. These divine energies are three measurements that can determine a person's stage of achievement.

On the level of human life, Tai Ching involves having a clean body: no sickness or dirty experience (or any dirty experience has been totally or spiritually cleansed through truthful personal growth.) Sang Ching refers to the clear mind which enables one to manage life with the surroundings in order to receive beneficial support. Yu Ching pertains to spiritual purity above all possible contamination by worldly life experience. It means the pure soul is enhanced by remaining intact and free any possible contamination of pressure internally or externally through life experience.

This goal of spiritual development is not what religions stand for, but a person might use any or all of the religions as material. What the achievement of the three goals involves, truthfully, is your being: the true situation and true reality of your being. There is no color or gender discrimination, no social background or worldly achievement necessary, and no minimum number of students or followers.

Q: Some highly achieved ones remain in high positions, not for their glory but for serving others, right? For example, I notice that worldly religious promotion is like the star system in the movies. A young girl may be trained and spend lots of money on advertisement to become a star, which makes it easier to become hired for a show. It is a tremendous financial investment for a new star.

But the real spiritual realm is not a star system. It is totally the opposite. The high spiritual realm of natural reality is definitely a level, criterion or a measurement of divinity. A divinely achieved being does not come to the world to take anything. He comes purely for the purpose of giving. He can manage himself and manage other things well, but most things are just a game. He helps people and helps the world, but does not describe himself as we used to hear, "I am the king of kings, I am the lord of lords."

Master Ni: People of the highest achievement are not definable. True achievement is unknowable. High achievement is unknowable and does not need to be proven to others. The purpose of the lovely fragrance of a flower is not to please people. It is natural, like a natural soul, simple and truthful. It still takes quite long for most students to conform their lives to the simple and plain truth of natural healthy living.

Note: This chapter can be read in conjunction with Master Ni's books, Internal Spiritual Growth Through Tao, Nurture Your Spirits, *and* Quest of Soul, *etc.*

Chapter 6

Realizing Heaven in Our Lives

I

Q: Master Ni, would you speak more about what you have taught us about spiritual sobriety and spiritual tipsiness?

Master Ni: Spiritual sobriety is retaining the ability to be attentive to and correctly responsive to one's environment, while at the same time meeting the needs of one's higher life goals (having a safe, healthy life and providing a supportive environment for one's spiritual practice and learning). This means doing a good job at work; doing your share and keeping correct behavior at home; being attentive to accomplishing one's tasks and alert to possible mistakes in the marketplace.

Spiritual sobriety is one of the spiritual goals I have talked about. It is a type of service to oneself and others. Spiritual traditions must agree that the path to Heaven is through service to others because the constancy of working correctly can be a mirror to show a person how he is doing. If he loses his sobriety, he knows it immediately because he sees errors arise in his work.

It is nice when you begin to see success in your cultivation of spiritual sobriety. There are fewer errors in work and daily life, you begin to learn how to handle the ones that do come up, and you feel good about yourself and your life. People respond to you differently; maybe some of them stop trying to avoid you so much, because you now have something to offer them. Also, some things bother you less or do not have the power over you that they did before. Your life has a greater richness, smoothness and positiveness to it. Your life begins to have a more heavenly quality to it.

I believe that spiritual sobriety is a good goal for many people. It is nice to describe it, but it is better to know how to start to achieve it. A person will achieve it by wanting it more than anything else. He just says to himself, "I want things to go well and right in my life at all times and in all situations," and then he begins to apply himself to seeing that it happens. Not just one day, but he reminds himself of his goal every day. Surely, no one can live a totally trouble-free life, but there is a certain point you reach where you know you are beginning to attain that goal of spiritual sobriety and balance. Just do not give up, no matter what happens in your life.

Spiritual tipsiness perhaps is not as easy to understand as spiritual sobriety.

Everybody needs some enjoyment in life. There are different kinds of enjoyment or "drunken feelings" possible in earthly life. There are those brought by drugs or alcohol, those brought by illusions or religions, those brought by emotions such as extreme happiness or sadness, those brought by ownership of material possessions or certain relationships, those brought by accomplishing moral actions, and those that are purely spiritual. Whatever good feeling we reach is a kind of tipsiness or drunkenness. All are a movement of energy, but the difference between them is what energy is moved, how the energy is moved and the amount of harm or harmlessness involved in moving it.

Spiritual tipsiness is the most excellent form of enjoyment because a person can do it and still maintain his sobriety and harmlessness. That is, a person can still meet all his obligations and responsibilities; perhaps he even does better at them. Spiritual tipsiness is not harmful to others or oneself. However, it is important for a person to learn the self-control and good lifestyle that is necessary to experience sobriety and tipsiness at the same time if they want the full delight. Tipsiness alone is not enough. It is so much more wonderful to have one's life going well externally and also have the good feeling of spiritual tipsiness or contentment.

It is nice to describe spiritual tipsiness, but it is better to learn how to attain it in one's life. You are always encouraged to learn it after you have attained spiritual sobriety or at the same time. It is done through constantly practicing awareness of the point between the nipples or heart center during all kinds of situations. For many people it is most easily experienced in quiet times alone, but practicing it at all times, when suitable to do so, brings more result. This type of concentration moves the energy out of the intellectual head into the heart and creates the pleasant feeling. It is when a person stops thinking. Having a quiet or unstressful life makes it easier to do, because a person's energy is already somewhat more contained within his body rather than scattered out in confused or unnecessary events.

Spiritual sobriety is manifest when a person applies his life energy to making the world better. It is a movement of energy from the person's being out to the world. Spiritual tipsiness is manifest when a person brings the energy back into his body to replenish himself. That makes it possible for him to continue to be around, to work with or serve other people in whatever way his life requires of him. It is the delightful movement of energy like the breath, in and out. When the two are balanced together, there is a perfection of being. I believe that a person who can attain both sobriety and tipsiness at the same time is what they call the perfect person. That does not mean that all is perfect in his external life, but that he is perfectly balanced within.

To be concise, spiritual tipsiness is applied to ignoring the errors of people who have wronged you, mistreated you and cheated you. It means forgiving people without even mentioning their mistake. It means not thinking about or remembering people's inconsiderate behavior. It means being insensitive to or ignoring irritations, provocations and meaningless challenges. Furthermore, it is not noticing people's ill manners or improper use of words to talk to you or about you, etc.

On many occasions in my teaching and writing, I promote maintaining clarity of mind. On this occasion, I would like to talk about its opposite in answering your question. As all of you know, truthfulness, exactness, precision, accuracy and being matter-of-fact, are very important for both spiritual intellectual learning and all general work.   In spiritual learning, unfortunately, the worldly convention is that the general spiritual teachings are ambiguous and lack clarity. People only repeat what people before them said, without knowing the source of such description. That type of situation is similar to this story: Once a man went from his rural home to go to town, and while he was there, he bought a fish. On the way home, he stopped to rest for a while under a tree, and so he hung the fish on one of the tree's limbs. Unintentionally, he fell asleep; he woke with a start, realized it was late and rushed off without taking the fish. It was not until he was already home that he remembered the fish. However, because some important household or business matters occupied his attention for several weeks, there was no chance for him to go back for the fish.

Later, on his next trip to the town, he overheard some people talking about a place outside their village where a new tree shrine was built, and where the tree god was efficacious and responsive. The tree was able to attract fish, so many people went over there to worship the tree and look for blessings. When he heard them talking, it stirred his curiosity, so later that day, he went over and to his amusement, it was the exact same tree he had hung the fish on! Many people were there, worshipping or admiring it. Finally, he expended much energy to explain what had happened the day he hung the fish there. All the people there laughed, and then everybody went on their way.

In many spiritual traditions or teachings, the minds of later generations have deliberated over something of a simple origin, and then they have made a big story out of it. This is how teachings are spread without clarity. This is why I call out for clarity in spiritual teaching and learning. It is important to cultivate one's spiritual clarity and mental clarity in spiritual learning.

However, on this occasion, I am not talking about shutting off clarity in spiritual learning, but rather about a kind of spiritual clarity that has a feeling to it similar to artificial drunkenness. I am not talking about the drunkenness of religious followers who have lost their clear vision because they are following something absurd or obscure. I am talking about the healthy, good use of spiritual tipsiness which can be cultivated after a person has achieved spiritual lucidity. I am talking about a person who clearly sees the nature of life and all different kinds of relationships. This is a person who can clearly understand the world's problems, but is still not discouraged; he has not lost warmth in worldly life. He does not give up all normal world relationships. He is not even intimidated by his contact with the harshness and cruelty of some people.

Once you take a long, long time and you have spiritual awakening in your sight, you have already attained the good knowledge about the world, life and people. Two possible attitudes of life might occur from that awakening. One, a person who is clear about the world, people and himself does not like the world or the people very much because they might be trouble-makers to other people and himself. That kind of clear-mindedness will become the negative fruit of life unless the person learns more deeply. That kind of attitude is like distilled water; which is not as nutritious as good natural water. So those people are like distilled water: they would not like to become dirty, pulled down or troubled by the world, so they keep themselves far away from it. They separate themselves from people by their clear-mindedness. However, by separating themselves from people, they miss the spiritual and nutritional value that they otherwise might have achieved. So that attitude more or less develops into self-care, self-love, self-respect, self-pride, self-interest or general selfishness. That kind of clearness has no spiritual value. Those people, after achievement of this kind of clear mind, will withdraw themselves to a narrow corner and close their minds. They are no longer open to anyone's problem.

The second kind of attitude from spiritual clarity is when a person also knows that the world and the people in it are all troublesome. A person knows that close relationships are mostly uninteresting, such as the relationship between father and mother, son and father, sister and brother, etc. Those relationships are sometimes false because people are so selfish and each one is involved in his own interests with nothing to share. However, even after totally understanding that, this type of person does not hold any kind of wishful thinking, great expectation or anticipation for his relationships, yet he is still courteous with them. He keeps the normalcy in the relationship by fulfilling his part without looking to see whether the other one has done likewise or not. That is spiritual kindness that comes from lucidity of the mind. It is applied by a kind of spiritual tipsiness that was promoted by the ancient Taoists. In many paintings of the

ancient Taoists called immortals, you will notice that they are
holding a cup or pot of wine in their hands. But it is not wine
brewed from any earthly product. The wine is brewed of
wisdom; the wine drinking is the spiritual symbol of a kind of
blurred vision that can be applied to an unpleasant situation
in which a person is pushed, stung or made to feel uncomfortable. How can any person accept such a difficult situation? A person can accept it easily when he allows himself to
be in a mood or mind of drunkenness by the kindness he has
brewed up. It is a true kindness, not the play of shrewdness.
When most people have tolerance, it is usually because they
have asked for something, are waiting for a reward or are
expecting something to be returned to them. So this gives
them tolerance. Taoist tolerance or patience, however, does
not come from waiting for material, emotional or mental
payment from a situation. That kind of tolerance or patience
requires a specially achieved psychological or emotional power
to create a self-transcendent atmosphere.

Let us say you are in an awkward situation, a place
where people do not like or respect you, or where people do
not give you support or help or whatever you need at that
time. In so great a difficulty, you may remain poised, not out
of numbness of feeling, but out of your clarity about the
nature of people.

Success and prosperity bring prestige, respect, gifts and
help. When you have money, the banks write you letters to
offer you loans. But when you really need money, there is no
bank voluntarily offering a loan, because banking is a
business, it is not a help. Do you understand what the
example means? In the world, not everybody is greatly
successful; not everybody has great prestige or prosperity.
Social vanity and worldly heroism are what most people all
fight for and struggle for.

The spiritually achieved ones do not admire social vanity
or worldly heroism. They respect the normalcy of life. They
achieve to the point of knowing that the normalcy of life
contains the highest spiritual value. They might become
successful and prestigious, but they do not move their focus
away from the normalcy of life. It is the main goal of their

lives. They are willing to be normal people and to live in a normal, rather than a special, way.

I am not talking about normal in the sense that modern people or newspapers define it externally: A person thirty-four years old who owns a house, has a wife and two cars, 2.4 children or whatever the average is nowadays, a dog and three goldfish. This is a pretty picture painted by someone's mind and that is average, not normal. I am talking about normal in the sense of living one's life as it is. A person does not have to prove himself as better than the other people or able to do better than his parents, hero of the world, savior of the universe or even meet the newspaper definition of the average guy. I am talking about not living a fantasy, but living your life as it is. Life as it is, is sometimes boring, uncomfortable or tedious, with lots of work and unpleasant environments, situations or people. Right? Hasn't that been your experience at times? So, how do they handle living an ordinary, normal life in the harsh world? You sometimes need a special thing. To endure being in the real world, some directly use alcohol or drugs, others turn to religious numbness, while some join a persecuting force to try to re-order or change the world. However, a Taoist uses a specially made wine he brews from his wisdom. To be able to allow the world to be harsh, people to be cruel and situations to push him, the effect of the Taoist special wine might be the great virtuous fulfillment of forgiveness. He forgives the trouble, forgives the world, and forgives any people who wrong or mistreat him. Taoists do not call it forgiveness, however. Calling it forgiveness is a dualistic level and also makes one's ego too big; it puts the other people lower than you so that they need you to forgive their error. It might be called "A Taoist's self-made tipsiness." This tipsiness and blurry vision keeps him from seeing the mistakes of others and the harm or loss to himself. He does not know how another has wronged him or how they have mistreated him. It is not that he does not see into it; he simply decides that he does not care about the small losses. He knows, but he does not care. There is something much more interesting going on, and he can afford to take the loss anyway because he has built up his strength. He is so wise, and because he is too kind, he looks like a simpleton who allows people to take advantage of him. He does not push hostility to the extreme.

However, in practical life, some people feel pain or agony because they are too serious about every small thing. Sometimes, a person should not be too critical or too clear about the details. The application of clarity or clear mind still requires a person's better management to know the right circumstance in which to apply it. So when one's spiritual tipsiness is applied to the right spot, it can be lubricating, useful or helpful. At least it can make one's legs stronger; a person can stand stronger with it. All of this is to say that when you give people an easier time, it is also giving yourself an easier time.

We really know nothing. All knowing is on the relative sphere. What is right as we define it is only relatively right. What we think is wrong is but relatively wrong. We really do not know the truth. We only know what is not truth, because all knowledge which can be established and recognized is in the relative sphere. Thus, how can anyone be assertive enough to declare he has reached the truth? The truth is no truth, because it transcends all knowledge that we know. You do not know, I do not know, and he does not know. That is the highest and the deepest we can know. If anybody says he knows, he does not know, because he admits it if he does not know something. He is not assertive if he is not sure of something. In reality, the truth is still known to the unknown mind. We do not know, but we follow the truth until we do not follow the truth and run into problems.

Truth is not instinct either. It is just the natural truth of all life. It is not an establishment. It is nature; a fish does not know why or how it can swim.

We usually take scientific knowledge as most truthful and accurate. You have received a scientific education, at least in school. It is knowledge, but it cannot be certain that it is all scientific. No knowledge is permanent knowledge. We think that truthful knowledge must be permanent. However, not all truthful knowledge is in written form. You can be sure, however, that the scientific knowledge you learned is not permanent because it has changed since you left school. Your parents and teachers wished you to learn all of it, but now it has all become out-of-date. Some might even think that the basics are invariable. But, as you know, they are a temporary standard which somebody set for the convenience of moving forward for the further probe. Thus, in science, nothing can be permanent. There are accepted suppositions. They are a language that is a way to establish a communication or pass around such information.

Then it comes to the last type of knowledge: you may think that mathematical knowledge is the most truthful. If that is so, then 1 + 1 = 2 must always be the same. In the real world, however, numbers and mathematics are really the most superficial. For example, somebody's one thousand dollars does not mean the same as your one thousand. Your two brothers are not the equals of someone else's two brothers. Every day you drive to a city and travel the same mileage. The meaning is very different from the same mileage which you cover in a different time and place.

My suggestion here is to not become judgmental or overly opinionated about the meaningless fight.

Nobody should think of himself as a nobody, or a somebody. You are nobody and somebody always at the same time. This level is not a place to establish your judgement. Reality has no emotional involvement. One should also be open to the reality that we cannot really 'know' anything, and that understanding that we cannot really 'know' except in a conceptually relative sense is the beginning of self-awakening.

Sometimes when I am talking about spiritual strength, I use the term spiritual sufficiency. The *Tao Teh Ching* calls it self-contentment from self-containment of natural life. The two concepts have the same meaning: a person who is strong spiritually and cannot be blown away like the wind or who does not collapse or panic in a difficult situation. An observer would say that such a person has self-confidence. That is mostly used as a general English word. If a person lacks confidence in himself, if he has no spiritual strength, he always feels that people are tramping on him, or that he is a nobody. He does not know that how he feels depends on how strong his spirit is, not even necessarily on external achievements that make a person "somebody" in the eyes of the world. A person with spiritual self-confidence or containment does not feel tramped upon, even when in a "losing" situation. On the spiritual level, we do not talk about confidence. Confidence is on more of a physical level. Both lack of confidence and over-confidence may be a source of trouble which invites mistakes.

Instead, to describe the spiritual level, we have used the words spiritual sufficiency or self-containment. With spiritual sufficiency, you feel you are born from nature, are a part of nature and stay with nature. You feel that you lack nothing and that you are able to fulfill your own life. You are not longing for the types of achievement that other people have had, you are not looking only to be the same as other people. If you go looking for other people's achievements, you are like a duck who is trying to sing like a lark. You feel disappointed that you cannot sing like a lark, but you do not see that you swim better than he does. Once a person knows his nature, he will be inclined to follow or identify with his nature.

There are so many people living so close to each other in this crowded world. People push other people, and people also imitate other people. The result is that they each lose their own nature. So, in this advice, I am saying that a person needs to do his best to fulfill his own nature, and thus learn to enjoy himself. How do you refine your own nature? By staying with yourself until you experience it. Then you will learn to enjoy yourself.

If Taoists have any special feature, it is that they know how to enjoy themselves in a difficult situation. A person can do many things that can change into a job or a means of earning money. Money has two sides to it. Of course it is a means for sufficiency and convenience in your life, which is positive. But it also has a negative side: it requires hard work to make it, and once you have it, you have to protect it from thieves, inflation, taxes, swindles, fraud, and your own careless handling.

For example, let us say that you are a person who is good at making money. You must learn to manage it, to protect and use it wisely and beneficially. As years go by, you will experience physical and emotional changes. You will experience relationships changing and the world changing. All change must happen; however, your money cannot stop all the changing, can it? If you know this, at least you know that money is not the goal of life; it is not a correct standard for support. There is no spiritual growth in merely pursuing or accumulating money without a higher goal.

What, then is the goal of life? The goal of life is the normalcy of life. However, who can keep one's life the same forever? There is a Taoist proverb that says, "Keep open to the world; at the same time, return to yourself." Is this possible? Yes; however, it is the way of reaching one's own innermost balancing point. It is the wisdom of life management. As I know, most Taoists were farmers, scholars or other people who lived decent lives. Some may question the word 'decent,' and ask, according to whom? Who sets the value on what is decent? Is the decency of the people who lived during the Middle Ages the same as that of modern people? Do people of different times and places think that decency is the same thing? To most people, decency means what is socially agreeable. Is what is socially agreeable really decent? For example, in previous epochs, if you took someone's daughter as your wife, you needed to pay a dowry to her parents. Otherwise, it was not a respectable marriage. Is that decent?

In different societies, do people really know the decency of life or do they just follow the cultural mode and religious customs? I am not talking about compromising on what is socially agreeable, but what is important and spiritual; I am talking about the secondary level of life; usually you do not have much freedom of choice. I am not talking about the spiritual decency of all times, all societies and all people. I am talking about what is momentarily in your life. It is obviously not right to bend your spiritual nature to society. Also, it seems you are unable to bend society to you. To achieve your important goal, you must follow the middle range which offers the highest flexibility in maneuvering but you still can confirm your life to the decency beyond temporal measurement. As the ancient sage taught, "In big things, one should not change one's virtue. On the small scale, flexibility is applicable." As to what is a big thing and what is small thing, can this be known by one's own moral knowledge? Yes, it can.

So by decent living, I mean honest labor, healthy handling of oneself and others. Is healthy handling the same as smart handling? As to the reality of the business world, my suggestion is to live with our solid peace of conscience, and not to undermine the peace of conscience by earning money through swindles, theft or fraud. So with regard to the ancient Taoists, most of them were farmers, scholars or people who lived decent lives. Whatever social or financial position they lived with, they enjoyed.

There are lots of good poems, all expressing how Taoists enjoyed themselves. Activities like T'ai Chi Movement, Chi Kung (Chi Gong), calligraphy, poetry or singing were not done to produce money. These things bring about happiness to the doer. Mostly we do it for self enjoyment and self amusement. If you do not do anything like the meditation of peaceful joy, you can still amuse yourself with the same mood which brews the meditation of peaceful joy.

Now, I have a big story to tell. Once a young Taoist went to New York to work and was ready to go back home to Los Angeles. He was returning to Los Angeles on the same airline that he took to New York. However, the person who made the airplane reservations did not tell him that there was a layover in Dallas on his return trip. Well, he got on the plane, sat in his seat, shut his eyes and blocked his ears and began to do his typical meditation of peaceful joy which could bring him into spiritual tipsiness. So he sat there, greatly enjoying himself. When the plane landed at the airport, the stewardess announced, "We have arrived." So he took his luggage and walked out into the airport. He went to the ticket counter, and because this fellow is related to me, he called my son to come pick him up at the airport. He waited there for a while, but nobody came. He called again, and the answer was that they had already sent someone to meet him.

However, after waiting a while longer, he began to get mad, so he went out to look for a taxi. He told the taxi driver, "Take me to Santa Monica." The taxi driver said, "No," and drove away. He felt rather strange that the taxi driver was so unfriendly, and wondered whether they did not want to take some one who was non-white. So he went back into the airport, decided to take a bus and began to look for information about which bus goes to Santa Monica. It was a busy terminal and there were many buses, so he began to try to figure it out. During his search, the stewardesses from the plane he was on came by and noticed that he was a lost boy. "What are you looking for?" they asked him. "I would like to take a bus so I can go home," he replied. "Where do you live?" they asked. "I live in Santa Monica," he answered. They told him, "This is not the right airport; you need to go back to take another plane." So four hours later, he arrived in Los Angeles.

When he was finally on the airplane back to Los Angeles, he thought it was impossible that such a thing could have happened. There was no sign that said "Welcome to Dallas." None of the people in the airport were wearing Texas cowboy hats, and nobody spoke with a Texas accent. How was it possible that it was Dallas? However, it was Dallas. He enjoyed his peaceful joy and the trip, but he should have applied it in the right situation. I am not sure that this fellow made a very good example of how to use spiritual tipsiness.

To be honest, it was me. However, I only misapply my meditation once or twice in a lifetime, or several lifetimes. Forgive me for my bad example.

My main message is that in human life you sometimes feel bitter with your husband, wife, children, parents or someone else. You should not be too clear about how they have wronged you or how they treated you or whether they do things you do not approve. You should rather forget their errors. Spiritual tipsiness helps do that. Because family relationships are natural relationships, it is hard to put them in a calculator. When you are dealing with matters regarding certain people, you had better be a little bit spiritually tipsy. Human relationship is different from spiritual learning, scientific study or experiment or fulfilling one's job obligations, where great accuracy, exactness and precision are needed. Sometimes you need to take a different approach with relationships. I do not know what you call it in English, but in Chinese we have a special term called the deepest kindness as the thickest graciousness or Huen Ho. Huen Ho is like the process of making rice wine; before it is distilled, it is a little thicker and more nutritious. On all occasions of difficulty in life, you need to be like the wine before becoming distilled and made thin. Now come the words to describe what the ancient Taoists valued: unadulterated originalness and unaffected purity. It is different from generally promoted social manners or the religiously commanded discipline and practice. Those are false limitations.

In spiritual learning, in one's personal spiritual achievement, it is necessary to learn the truth and reject the untruth. Take the essence to nurture your soul. Do not consume the dregs, because they have nothing with which to nurture your soul. Those dregs are feed for pigs. In China, we have all kinds of wine; some people use rice to make wine and others use peanuts, sweet potatoes or many kinds of fruit. Taking the essence is nutritious and tasteful, but the dregs are usually just fed to the pigs. This is an important example because we learn how to nurture our mind, spirit and body by taking the essence but not the dregs.

Many people live in a condition of much luxury, with a high material standard. Other people cannot achieve that. There is no need to build up jealousy for those who are more fortunate. Those with greater material fortune work harder to achieve that or else it is their personal destiny. It is a temporary reward with no lasting value. It is one's interest and destiny. However, the real reward in life is spiritual enjoyment, and that is not necessarily connected to one's material destiny. Spiritual enjoyment and spiritual achievement are like really good wine; there is no place where you can buy them. This high essence is something that you brew.

All things have their purpose according to how they are applied. For example, Oriental people think ginseng is a highly nutritious herb. This is true, but of course its usefulness depends on the situation to which it is applied. It is helpful, for example, to a mother who is delivering a baby and who loses lots of blood. On that occasion, when the mother keeps a piece of the ginseng root in her mouth at the right time and sucks on it, it will supply her with lots of strength and help to stop the bleeding. This is a right occasion to use ginseng. It is extra energy. Generally speaking, the energy we rely on for our everyday activity or for our basic health and longevity is not extra energy; it is our own energy, the energy that we produce ourselves through our healthy lifestyle of good air, nutritious food, proper exercise, balanced emotions and positive activity. Whatever vitamins or minerals come from the sun, water or food you eat, all need to be transformed into energy by your own body. The best high nutrition is produced by yourself. It is a process of transformation.

I would like to give an illustration of how we use or transform spiritual nutrition. For example, let us say that you read a book, attend a class or learn something from a teacher. You have heard or read about it, but still you need to transform what you have read or heard to make it useful and nutritious to your own life. There are lots of people who hear or read about good things, but they do not do anything with this information, so there has been no grounding or application of the wisdom received. So you are the one who basically produces the nutrition for yourself by applying what you have learned. It is you also who produces whatever you need to sustain yourself in your life.

On the material level, a person makes money, buys food, cooks the food and eats it. Almost everything that you take from outside requires some kind of system to extract and transform the nutrition to make it useful for your life. In Taoism, we use the illustration of wine-making to describe this transformation that occurs in our bodies. So learning Taoism is much different from learning general religious teaching which promotes spiritual obscurity and ambiguousness. Taoism promotes spiritual clarity and tipsiness at the same time.

Religious teachers will tell you that when you go out in the world, you need to be like a snake or fox. A Taoist is totally the opposite of a snake or a fox. Spiritually, you have to attain high lucidity, but in worldly matters, you cannot be too picky, too critical or too judgmental. You can be judicious, but not judgmental. Put your life into brewing to produce the essence for yourself, but not into the stage of already being the leftover dregs. We keep brewing to produce the new essence or new energy. Yet we do not exhaust all the systems of our life being. We enjoy all of what we have produced, but do not stop the function to take new material from producing new essence.

You need to understand the image of the eight immortals. They were together with all different kinds of people, enjoying themselves. They have lived in the world, but at the same time, they were not attached to the world. It means they live in it but they are not caged or entrapped by their achievement. They maintain their freedom to move through all different kinds of environments.

We really do not necessarily worship or honor a person who already lives in the mountains, is already high in heaven, or has already finished with all the trouble of worldly life. That is a dead example promoted by the worldly religions. That is not a good example to those who are still entrapped, still alive in the world. We make an example of people who still live in the world but are not entrapped by the world. This type of person can live in a relationship, but not be entrapped by them. I am talking about all kinds of relationships, boy/girlfriend, business, government, social; any type of human relationship. That is what we value. The shiens are free spiritual people. They are happy people. They are people who have not put a stop to enjoying their achieved spiritual happiness or spiritual freedom. Thus, they are called immortals. Being immortal is a spiritual achievement.

Practically, this means that worldly life has a type of bondage or a molding pattern. Each society has its system. No person can avoid all kinds of conventional regulations and the like. But the people who are achieved are not bothered by any of it. They comply with it, but are not inextricably tied to it. They respect it, but they do not worship it.

I deeply respect the examples of the ancient achieved ones. Most people admire the shiens because they think that the shiens have nothing to do but sit around and enjoy themselves. People sitting around is a kind of obstructive spiritual image that blocks the development of their admirers. The real shiens are the ones just like yourself, who have the courage to live in a world that seems not to make any great progress. But they are not intimidated; they are here to work out any possible problem.

A heavenly kingdom or spiritual paradise is not built in the air. A heavenly kingdom is not our imagination. What a spiritually achieved person does is to make himself, his own environment and his contacts less critical, picky and cruel, and more friendly and accepting. At the same time, he works to improve himself, his environment and his contacts so that there is less to criticize. All this is to make the world a real paradise. People who are unachieved would never find that type of heaven a beautiful paradise at all. They think it is too much work. Paradise, a heavenly kingdom, happens to those who are willing to achieve themselves in their lives and never be intimidated or discouraged by difficulty in life.

The world is every person's business. Each person's life can improve the world. The hope of the world is not realized by a religion, it is accomplished through individual spiritual realization. That means no self-cheating or no self-deception. With clarity, we know where we go. Broad or uncritical acceptance smooths frictions and conflicts that would otherwise happen in everyday life. Spiritual maturity brings about avoidance of small frictions and conflicts. Everyone's spiritual health increases in the group when one person's spiritual health increases. Heaven is the practical spiritual achievement of one person; then his friends, environment and people he contacts are all benefitted by his growth. At least he is not the one who plays tricks or mistreats people.

Let heaven be with you, the world, all religions and all spiritual leaders. Let them look for clarity; clarity is clear knowledge about spiritual reality. Do not use false hope which has been misapplied psychologically by unscrupulous individuals to take advantage of undeveloped people. Let heaven be with the political leaders. Let heaven be with everyone.

In my books and teaching, I advocate that all of you become good people. How do you apply those principles of being good in your daily life? There is a unique way. Before you are totally achieved, I believe you will be looking for understanding. By reading whatever I have taught, you can attain a general understanding. That is good enough. Those understandings will work automatically during specific occasions when you need them. You might like to give up your hostility, and give other people a break. You may ask me, But what about other people? I want them to give up their hostility. My answer is this: If we wish to be Taoists, persons of unadorned truth, we have got to be thorough Taoists. We cannot ask or demand such things of other people; we can only demand that we ourselves do them.

So how do we change ourselves? We do it situation by situation. Before doing something, we always ask ourselves, can we afford this action? We need to check out ourselves and our positions first. Can we afford to have people mistreat, wrong, trick or cheat us? If we can afford it, we do it in a relaxed mood. Some very wise people look very foolish at times because it appears that the other person is cheating them. But perhaps in that instance it is their kindness that is giving help to the other one.

For example, your friend wishes to borrow some money from you. In this case, you are in a good situation financially so loaning the money would be no problem. This person then mentions something you would like him to do for you as bait to make you decide to loan him the money. He is trying to have psychological influence on you. So what can you do in response? Do you respond to the bait or respond to his need? You want to make the balanced, correct decision. You must look at the reality of whether in this instance, it is wise that you lend the money to the person. Does the friend have the ability and the integrity to pay you back? You might not even care about that and still wish to loan the money to help your friend. But you would do that only if you can afford the loss if he does not pay you back. But whatever you decide, never base your decision on the friend offering to do the nice thing for you. That could be a social skill, or it could be that the person just knows what you like. Do not let people influence you; just learn to make your own decisions for your own good reasons.

When unfavorable things happen to a thorough person of truth, as when someone does not pay back the money borrowed, then he is not upset or surprised because he had the foreknowledge that such a thing might occur. He expected it might possibly happen. Thus he has the strength to deal with the situation. He does not avoid the unpleasant outcome. He does not escape it. He lets the thing happen because he knew it might be a possible outcome and he was willing to take that risk. So, he never comes back to complain about it.

If a person is only half achieved, he had better not take risks. Such risks are too much trouble or too painful for him. He pays a price, but he does not get what he wanted. Mostly all spiritual teaching, if it is normal spiritual teaching, promotes people to do good and to be good. In judging a teaching, it is important to look at the source. Do the teachers do good? All spiritual teachers take their teachings from the ancient spiritual knowledge, so you can judge their application of their teaching by how they live their lives. Surely, people can make mistakes. However, people can grow from their mistakes if the teaching and the learning material is right and reaches the truth. There is no guarantee that the people who teach chastity and purity with their words actually live that way or that they will live by it exactly. They call sexual activity a sin, but in practical life, if you look at it, you might discover that they commit the sins they condemn.

Do not look at other people to see how they are doing. If you look at other people, you might become discouraged. Look at yourself. If you choose to be a good person, you do not need to look at or imitate other people. Just be what you are. We are so crowded today in city life, in school life and in society; people are everywhere. For example, if a person works for a company, he more or less influences other people. People imitate others in their way of talking or treating people. How can you be a kind person, displaying your original nature in the midst of our commercial, highly structured society? You probably think that you cannot, but you can. If you want to know how to reach that goal, do the following: Stop and examine yourself; examine what part of your attitudes and reactions to things is only imitations of your parents, brothers, sisters, fellow students or work colleagues. You may find that what you picked up from them is not the way you want to be.

Check it out. You are looking for your personal original nature. You might find that spiritual happiness, contentment and sufficiency come from your own true nature; it does not come from imitation. For example, two people work in the same company. Whatever kind of car the first one buys, the second one buys the same kind or better. Whatever kind of lifestyle the first one has, the second one has to have the same kind or better. That is imitation and competition. That type of behavior never ends. Imitation and competition are not spiritual freedom. Whenever one person imitates another, maybe for one moment he thinks it is happiness, but that happiness is not his own standard or decision. It is somebody else's standard. For example, leather shoes are shiny and tai chi shoes are not. They have different functions. Buying shoes is not a matter of which is shiny or not, but depends on the use of the shoes. If you live or work in certain places, maybe there is a standard for dressing. If there is no standard, you would perhaps rather find something that suits you well, something that makes you feel really supported and happy. Often when a woman sees another woman decorate herself with cosmetics or jewelry, she goes to imitate it. It is a fashion, and she feels happy about it. But that happiness is short-lived. Do not let a social fashion become the truth of life.

I do not say there is a downfall of human morality. We are looking for the inner strength of life. We cannot worship the external standard of a colleague or a famous star all of the time. So, just do what you can do. Be what you really are. Correct the mistakes you have been making, straighten up the misunderstandings within yourself and with the people in your surroundings. Usually, external circumstances do not need to be straightened at all; if you try to straighten them, sometimes it just causes more trouble. So do not try to straighten things, but just be your real self. Do you really know your real self? You do not know, because your thoughts and emotions are already programmed by your society, family and cultural background. But there is a way that you can express your true self within the context of your society, family and cultural background. You need to look for the truth of nature.

I have mentioned that a duck does not need to envy the singing of a lark and wish to have that skill. Nor does the lark need to learn to swim as well as the duck. They are different birds.

World progress, individual personal progress can be made by simple steps. Be truthful with yourself. Be a thorough student of Tao, the natural harmony. It is not a big secret. Just choose to live a grassroots standard of reality of life and emotion. Those who truly live with a real heart are not those who live with the psychology of false hope promoted by religions. Religions continue to feed the bubble which might easily pop or break. People have lots of illusions because their false culture and their religion with its false spiritual teachings all promote illusion. You feel good about the teaching of religion for a while, but you never can reach it because the thing is not real; it is a bubble. Once you turn out to be an earnest being of nature, how happy you become. This is a simple thing that many knowledgeable people who know about religions do not know. Instead, they worship so many deities, so many gods to help them.

However, this is not my personal offering. All of the ancient achieved ones have told us these things. They have told us because we have deviated from the simple truth to the pull of external attraction for too long and too much. Once we courageously turn away from external attraction to rejoin ourselves, our spiritual natures, here we are, as complete as nature. We have reached this point, but we do not stay; instead we move forward.

II

Q: Master Ni, we know that the word "Tao" means "the Way." What is the origin of that word?

Master Ni: Tao is an ancient culture. Correctly termed, Tao is ancient natural spiritual education. It was a spiritual development of the ancient wise ones. Because Tao was so reputed and respected, the later unspiritual leaders also used the word Tao in their teachings. So there came to be two kinds of things called Tao: the true Tao and the false Tao. Tao practically means the Way. Therefore, we can call those two things the true Way and the false way. It is similar to money; there is true money and there is also counterfeit, which is also used by some people. There are some people who dare to do such things.

Because I am a student and an admirer of the ancient developed ones, I am responsible for what I am promoting. If my students do not know the truthfulness of Tao, then they will be fooled by the false Tao. The benefit of learning the truth of Tao is that it does not harm you. Tao does not cost anything. It does not ask you to pay for it. However, the false teaching always has a motivation behind it. The teaching of truth, though, does not make you belong to anyone; it guides you back to your own spiritual nature and universal nature. It makes you belong to yourself. That is the first thing to remember when somebody offers to teach you Tao. You have to understand the motivation or the truthfulness of the learning itself.

In this point, for the purpose of avoiding confusion, I would like to tell you where the culture of the spiritual education of Tao came from. It is necessary to remember the book called the *Tao Teh Ching*. You also need to know the source or background of the *Tao Teh Ching*: its teachings come from the *I Ching*.

We all have some knowledge about the *I Ching*. There are sixty-four hexagrams. The first hexagram is called Heaven, the Creative Energy of Heaven or the Creative Energy of Nature. During the Zhou dynasty, the order of the hexagrams was changed to make Heaven the first one.

Before and after the Zhou dynasty, the great leaders of each epoch worked on the *I Ching*, and each put something more in it to further develop the understanding of the *I Ching*. So you see that the original *I Ching* was not one version; there were at least three different versions. For example, the *I Ching* was initiated by Fu Shi. Then Shen Nung and then the Yellow Emperor worked on it further. During the Hsia Dynasty (2205-1766 B.C.), it was entitled *The Continuous Mountains*. During the Yin Dynasty (1766-1123 B.C.), it was entitled *The Great Collection* and during the Chou Dynasty (1122-249 B.C.), it was entitled *Chou's Book of Changes*.

At the time when Fu Shi wrote it, the order of the *I Ching* was different; the first hexagram was not Heaven or Chien. It was K'un, the Receptive Energy of Nature. So the first chapter or first hexagram originally taught one to be receptive. The way of K'un or the Way of Being Receptive is the translation or interpretation of Tao, the Way.

First of all, the ancient spiritual vision did not think that people were masters of the world or of the universe. They knew that universal nature or the nature of the universe was the main strength, main force and main leadership of the entire world. For example, can we choose to be born or not be born? We cannot. Basically, we are in a receptive position. Also, humans have a time to come and a time to go. We have a time to prosper and a time to transfer to a more hidden stage. Thus, we see that there are cycles to universal nature.

To be fully human is to learn to be wise. Learning to be wise is learning to be receptive to what happens in the cycles of life. And being wise is learning to cope with external change in a better way. So the K'un Tao, or Receptive Tao, means to be as receptive and accepting as a minister, a wife, a mother, a son, a daughter or a citizen. This is the duty or the rule of all ordinary human people. For example, we can use the terms minister, wife, etc., as illustrations. Though we can be creative in many capacities to take care of assigned work and to accomplish whatever comes to our hands, we are sometimes in positions which we would not choose. Life itself is not what we choose; we are only receptive to being formed and reformed.

So if you have interest, you can study the second hexagram in today's order of the book, K'un; then you will understand what Lao Tzu teaches and what the *Tao Teh Ching* teaches. The *Tao Teh Ching* originated before the Yellow Emperor.

What Confucius taught much later is lots of established dogma. During his time, people had the ambition of self aggrandizement. They wished to expand their ideas and impose them on other people, all with the ambition to influence and group others. That type of life is what we call being used by the natural impetus or natural impulse. It always keeps doing, but it has no eyes or vision to see the results of its actions, because the natural potency or natural impulse is also blind impulse. However, when a person is receptive, then he has the eyes to see, to know and to choose correct action.

So the *Tao Teh Ching* appears to have some unusual teachings, but that is only because they are not easily understood. For example, the book says to keep yourself in a weak condition. Or it says to keep yourself in a soft position, like an old hen, a valley riverbed or a ravine. People do not understand what the book means, so we can make an example of the moon to illustrate what it means.

Life in ancient times had more connection with nature and its cyclic movement. Nature takes on cyclic curves and becomes a rhythmic movement. Surely we can say that when we experience the darkness of night, we know that we shall soon enjoy dawn and the brightness of the day. When we suffer from the bitterness of the winter cold, it means the warmth of spring will soon come. Nature always provides opportunity for life to return. Death in nature always means that life will return.

I mentioned the example of the moon. When the new moon, shaped like an eyebrow, starts shining in the sky and we see it, we know that it will soon be a full moon. In seeing the fullness of the moon, we know its light will soon decline. When the waning of the moon comes, then it will soon turn into the dark part of the cycle. So each part lets us know that the next part is about to arrive.

So the main teaching of the *I Ching* is to not overstretch or overexpand yourself. Why does it teach that so repeatedly? Because once you expand yourself to your highest or fullest point, it means you will finish with that and move on to your lowest point. Therefore the *Tao Teh Ching* teaches you to remain weak, soft and not fully grown, like a ravine, a valley, a woman or a hen. It means you always keep a low position, remain in a certain stage of a cycle. In that stage, you give yourself room for more growth.

When Fu Shi first decided that nature is a development, he divided all development into three stages. The first stage is the beginning, the middle stage the time of achievement or fulfillment and the third stage the overly used strength or the overly done. When the eight trigrams were developed into sixty-four hexagrams, six stages of division were brought about. Each hexagram is two sets of development, three stages each. When they are combined, the second and the fifth lines are where the balance is usually seen. The third and the sixth lines still express a situation of overly done or too much.

The general religious teaching is to go to heaven, to become rich or to attain high prosperity. But once you attain that point, where will you go? In a cyclic movement, when a bow is fully stretched before shooting an arrow, it means that in the next stage it must spring back. If overstretched, the bow may break. My friends perhaps will wonder: if you can keep the position of the sprung back stage, then why can't the position of fullness be kept? You cannot because the developing force of a bow takes two sides of pressure: external and also internal. It cannot be kept because the stretched stage has two forces to it: the internal force of the bow trying to contract and the external force of the person stretching it. There is no way to keep the original point, at least not in personal growth. This is to suggest you not overstretch your life for things without true value. Otherwise, you are like an overstretched bow that takes pressure from both sides. This wears out your life spirit.

So the teaching of the *Tao Teh Ching* comes from the hexagrams of the *Book of Changes*, especially the hexagram called K'un, which was the first hexagram in the original order.

So always remain young. A young person is usually weaker than a fully developed adult. For example, let us say that somebody has made a million dollars, and believes that he has already achieved his top performance. He has no more to do. Let us say another person has made a hundred million; he does not consider himself finished, because he still has lots of potential to go. This is similar to the story of a girl who was just given a cow. She got a bucket of milk from it, and put the bucket on her head to carry. She began to daydream about what she would do with the money from the sale of the milk. Immediately she could see the beautiful clothes on her body, and imagined that she was invited to a dance. She was admired by many people at the party, and so she walked and looked aside at them, turning her head - and thus the bucket of milk on her head spilled onto the ground and her party was spoiled.

People who have reached spiritual depth and breadth are not easily exhausted. The *Tao Teh Ching* hints that when many people have become too strong or too proud, they then push or force others. They are small people, or at least they are small containers. By this I mean that they are easily filled by whatever they attain and become proud. A little knowledge, and immediately they think, "I am the king. I am the king of kings." But they have become such bullies. Someone else would say, "I am the greatest teacher in the entire world. My teaching is useful all the time." But his teachings are limited, because he has limited growth, no big growth.

In the *Tao Teh Ching*, there is not much formality. It only reveals the truth we might like to comply with in order to attain more. Spiritual education teaches internal spiritual unification. Because one's life has so many elements outside and inside, spiritual unification is very important. Other words that describe it are spiritual unity. The first chapter of *Tao Teh Ching* teaches spiritual unity. The second chapter of the *Tao Teh Ching* teaches counter-balance of the common relative reality presented by inter-assistance and inter-accomplishment between opposites. The concluding, finishing part of the *Tao Teh Ching* teaches that the most important thing, learning, attainment, growth is a good, earnest life and gives instruction on how to attain it. The entire teaching of the *Tao Teh Ching* was based on the *I Ching*. The *Tao Teh Ching* teaches that the fulfillment of natural good life. All good virtues are contained in a good life. When the good virtue of natural good life is fulfilled, that is the Heavenly way.

The Heavenly Way of life means to balance your own life. You have to learn enough so that you have something to give. If you do not learn anything that you can do yourself, how can you have something to give? In today's time, people want to give, but they do not learn enough first before they start. In my teaching, every question that comes along, comes more and more to the point. As contrast, when I first came to the

West; people asked questions that were more troubled; they had suffered from a certain living environment. I believe that once we learn the great principles from the *Tao Teh Ching*, all the answers can be attained and put to use naturally, in the small situations, in the small situations.

The teaching in the *Tao Teh Ching* is not like any limited religion that talks about going to Heaven. Each religions talk about heaven, but they are competitive because they would all like to be heaven. Rather than being heaven, they are expressing the untamed animal nature of humans themselves. Religions are disguised competitive forces for social influence. But the imagined God of their religions cannot last. What do I mean? Even God or gods that stretch their influence into the sphere of tai chi must experience the cycle of expansion and shrinking, rise and fall. There is no exception. All the competitive teachings have a chance to gather lots of people, a chance to gather understanding and support for a time, a chance to fall. But time changes and life changes. If you understand change, you are receptive. But those assertive teachings cannot accommodate the changes.

You are students of Tao; learn to be receptive. From different changes, you can retain your best as new lives, never worn out. Even at an old age, Lao Tzu declared, "I am not born yet, I am still in my mother's womb." But many people are going to be assertive even before they have reached their maturity. So then trouble in the world comes from competition among them. The competitors do not see that they will be washed away by the changes.

The Taoists sit at the side of the ocean and see one wave after another attacking the rocks of the shore. We say that yang energy, which is natural potency or the natural impulsive force, is just like the waves which come from the ocean, are formed by the ocean, and rush to the shore where they meet the rocks. They create a big noise, a whoosh, a splash of water, a crash; and then the water goes away. The waves come, again and again.

Spiritual development comes from quiet observation, like the one who sits on the shore, watching the waves. Surely any person can play in the waves, riding on waves like the surfer. The one who does that will then experience the up and down, the standing up and falling in the water. You are young, so you enjoy it. However, the natural cycle, the cyclical movement of nature must be understood. In nature, human history or in an ordinary human life, nothing can avoid the cyclical pattern of movement whether you are a believer in a religion or not. Before the ultimate law of Tai Chi, such fantasy is of no use. No person should work to speed up the stages of the cyclical sections, but should instead slow down the natural speed of the spiral. One can only work for his spiritual development to transcend the cyclic nature of the earth plane.

The religions of the later generations talk about reincarnation and about saving the soul, all with no real effect. The *Tao Teh Ching* and the *I Ching* always tell us: Nature gives birth to life. Life shall ride the new cycle to come back again. This continues all the time. A tree falls; it dies. Then a new tree will grow. An island will burn to ashes, but all new life, animals, birds and vegetation will come back again. The seeds of human life are in the subtle level as spirits. They are not seen like the seeds of vegetation. Souls are the seeds of life of human people. When you are in physical life, maintain your subtle seeds of life well, so you will always have a chance to come back and live again.

In general, religions tend to take a section of reality as the whole cycle. Thus, they look at the downward or ending part of the cycle of life as the whole thing. Student of Tao, however, keep their focus on the fact and knowledge of wholeness that whatever dies returns to live newly. Renewal of life is the knowledge of the students of Tao; they are not stuck by death. By this I mean that the living faith of students of Tao make death a small part of the eternal cycle. They nurture the force of continuous living; they remain young in spirit in all lives.

[*This chapter is reprinted from Master Ni's book,* Internal Growth Through Tao.]

Chapter 7

Reaching Spiritual Unity

The first book I worked on was *The Complete Works of Lao Tzu*. Some of my students' growth in understanding made them ready for the height of Lao Tzu. Lao Tzu's teaching is the account of a person who has already reached the top of the mountain and has seen all the surroundings clearly, but who, with his own understanding, lives an ordinary life among ordinary people.

Taoism as a religion was mistakenly understood to be the worship of leisure, a trouble-free life of merry-making, freedom and tremendous enjoyment. Is that true? It is true in a sense, but not in the way you might think. It is a special achievement after long years of working on yourself until the day neither you nor the world is your trouble. That does not mean that you do not work, do not have trouble, or that you revel in luxury. It means that you become so efficient at working that work becomes your leisure, you become so capable at handling trouble that you can be merry while taking care of things, that your spiritual freedom of joy transcends any physical limitations of time or space that you might have, that you enjoy the good things that come to you as a part of your work. You are not discouraged about doing what you need to do. Enjoyment comes from spiritual achievement through hard work; it does not come from imagination or as a free gift of having faith in someone who is more powerful than yourself, someone who will help you or take away your troubles caused by lack of growth.

Some students have an idea that spiritual teaching is like taking some special drug to make them stoned. Drugs and similar things are, however, opposite from Taoist achievement. So many need to go back to learn the fundamentals which make a good life approachable and achievable by personal spiritual improvement. The book, *The Heavenly Way*, contains the main teaching entitled, "Tai Shan Kan Yin Pien." When I was a teenager, it was how I started to learn Tao. It was the foundation of people of Tao for many past generations. At the beginning, "Tai Shan Kan Yin Pien" was not appreciated by some of my students. However, because these students were still attached to the energy in my surroundings, it took a while for some of them to find their own way. Most of that group of students could have taken the teachings and worked hard to improve themselves spiritually. This teaching is practical as spiritual cultivation. The *Heavenly Way* received great response from other readers.

The book *Tao, the Subtle Universal Law* is an elucidation of the *Heavenly Way*, an essential spiritual work. It earns great appreciation in different Western countries. People who read the Heavenly Way and follow its guidance find that their lives improve.

With so many people's spiritual awakening and support, we have great hope to see spiritual improvement, and the possibility of spiritual progress and achievement of the entire human society. Progress can only be attained when differences in cultural background and different spiritual customs are not an issue in people's relationships. People shall meet each other shoulder to shoulder, hand to hand, to work out common human problems to attain Heaven in the world. I received the spiritual mission from our ancestors: it is the Heavenly Way as the goal of our spiritual realization. All our spiritual friends shall clearly know that is our spiritual direction.

The world has changed and people have opened up their eyes since World War II. They have discovered that conventional religion or faith does not work for all time and all people. It does not hold the absolute truth; it may only be helpful in a relative sphere. So people pose the questions: What, then, is the absolute truth? What is the ultimate law? They start to search for the answer. In this way, the young generation of Western society started to open up to welcome what could be offered from all corners of the world.

However, after examining some Oriental religions, some people of depth discovered that the response from the conventional religious practices, Oriental or Western, did not really answer their questions. The Viet Nam War especially made the young American generation interested in the teaching of Chuang Tzu. They esteemed it because they could find liberation from social pressure in his book, and also in the book, *Poems Written on the Cold Mountain*. Some Japanese Zen monks offered the Western world old Zen teachings to fill the gap of spiritual emptiness. However, Zen teaching is only one aspect of the teaching of Tao. Its real source is Tao. Thus, Tao started to receive attention.

Those young minds had not reached the deep appreciation of the teaching of Tao. The students had an incomplete impression of the teaching of Tao, and needed a solid foundation or different understanding of the teachings of this tradition of ultimate truth. The teaching of Tao guides people to become spiritually responsible, rather than dependent, which is what happens when people follow the surface level of conventional religions.

Through a little more than 2,000 years, human relationships have become even closer than before. People slowly work out their self-nature and no longer follow the thoughtless habit of imitation. Customarily, religion, commerce, fashion and social habits are developed by imitation. The political systems are also developed by imitation; politics is the strongest, most influential factor of all.

Imitation is animal nature. With the spiritual and intellectual growth of human people, imitation can still be practical; however, it is best to do so with wise and careful selection. Using modern China as an example, when it lost its confidence in the nature of its own evolution, political leaders eagerly imitated Western politics. This imitation did not help dissolve any of China's problems, so some time later, new Chinese leaders eagerly swallowed the system of their northern neighbor, Russia, and transplanted it into China. That did not help the Chinese problem either.

All people and all leaders of China failed to follow one important guideline: each existence must find its own nature. In that way, it can best attend to what is of common importance to all.

For slightly more than 2,000 years, the unnaturally built monarchy and the later one-party ruling system were used to control the masses. These types of governmental hierarchies are unnatural. So is the so-called "national socialism" which contains the elements of monarchy within a one-party ruling system.

During this last fifteen years, people have widely awakened to be able to see that no one society or one nation can solve all the problems of the human world. Nothing great will happen unless great cooperation is brought about by all societies, nations and individuals. This starts with spiritual awakening and not withholding narrow religious or national prejudice. This openness and broadness of spirit is similar to Tao.

I would not say the teaching of Tao in story form helps the world, although it may do some explanatory work. However, the spirit of Tao - restoring one's personal spiritual nature and being broadly open to differences has encouraged the world to come to a new epoch.

In some societies and nations, the spiritual growth of human people is greater and faster than in others. Therefore, the world, nations and societies which have attained more spiritual growth must help the societies, nations, and leaders who have less spiritual growth or development. It is the same thing in a small family or a community: the spiritually more developed always need to help the less developed ones with problems and disturbance.

It is improving oneself and growing spiritually, and then helping others which brings true enjoyment in life. The positive goal and new spiritual direction for this new generation is to look for the spiritual development of the entirety of human society.

Do not expect one powerful human being to become a savior of the world. That is an old type of thought. It is not practical.

We have experienced the difficulty and trouble of religious competition. This is why the teaching of Tao suggests that all artificial structures which are external attractions and are a tool for grouping people should dissolve and retreat to be secondary, even tertiary, elements of spiritual teaching. The emphasis of a single religious standpoint and the exaltation of those who imitate small religions with most powerful emotional strength, should transfer their strength to promote the god of no name and the god of all names. All religions could work together to help human society attain spiritual growth instead of emphasizing the teaching of religious prejudice.

In the ancient society, literature was respected. One book by a teacher could become popular and acceptable and could organize new strength. However, this old way of religion and politics does not help the world. It is mostly imitation. Imitation sometimes can cause people to become trapped. Is Islam not an imitation of Judaism? Is Judaism not an imitation of the religion of Babylon? The same habit of imitation also happens in the spiritual world of the Orient. New religious leaders of conventional teaching stand high on the platform to teach something nobody can prove. This kind of teaching can support a teacher's personal life through taking advantage of people's spiritual undevelopment. But that can never help the world. All teach the truth which cannot be colored, described or expressed. Tao is not able to be described; only from your deep spiritual nature can you find such subtle truth. You will find it once your energy is refined from the coarse level to be crystal clear.

Most people are happy to see that the world has been changed by the spiritual ancestors who respond to their meditation. The spiritual ancestors subtly guide new leaders in the human sphere to see more clearly, to understand better and to move in a new direction. It is people's responsibility to help each other abandon the conceptual narrowness of racism, nationalism, individual heroism and to convert or change to the practice of the broadness and openness of Tao.

About Taoist Master Ni, Hua Ching

Master Ni, Hua-Ching is fully acknowledged and empowered as a true Master of Tao. He is heir to the wisdom transmitted through an unbroken succession of 74 generations of Taoist Masters dating back to 216 B.C. As a young boy, he was educated within his family and then studied more than 31 years in the high mountains of China, fully achieving all aspects of Taoist science and metaphysics.

In addition, 38 generations of the Ni family have practiced natural Taoist medicine. Master Ni has continued this in America with clinics and the establishment of Yo San University of Traditional Chinese Medicine.

As a young boy, Master Ni, Hua-Ching was educated by his family in the spiritual foundation of Tao. Later, he learned Taoist arts from various achieved teachers, some of whom have a long traditional background. Master Ni worked as a traditional Chinese doctor and taught Taoist learning on the side as a service to people. He taught first in Taiwan for 27 years by offering many publications in Chinese and then in the United States and other Western countries since 1976. To date, he has published about 18 books in English, made five videotapes of Taoist movements and wrote several dozen Taoist songs sung by an American singer.

Master Ni stayed about 31 years in the mountains in different stages. He thinks the best way to live, when possible, is to be part-time in seclusion in the mountains and part-time in the city doing work of a different nature. He believes this is better for the nervous system than staying only in one type of environment.

The 50 books that Master Ni has written in Chinese include 2 books about Chinese medicine, 5 books about Taoist spiritual cultivation and 4 books about the Chinese internal school of martial arts. The above were published in Taiwan. He has also written two unpublished books on Taoist subjects.

The other unpublished 33 books were written by brush in Chinese calligraphy during the years he attained a certain degree of achievement in his personal spiritual cultivation. Master Ni said, "Those books were written when my spiritual energy was rising to my head to answer the deep questions in my mind. In spiritual self-cultivation, only by nurturing your own internal spirit can communication exist between the internal and external gods. This can be proven by your personal spiritual stature. For example, after nurturing your internal spirit, through your thoughts, you contact many subjects which you could not reach in ordinary daily life. Such spiritual inspiration comes to help when you need it. Writings done in good concentration are almost like meditation and are one fruit of your cultivation. This type of writing is how internal and external spiritual communication can be realized. For the purpose of self-instruction, writing is one important practice of the Jing Ming School or the School of Pure Light. It was beneficial to me as I grew spiritually. I began to write when I was a teenager and my spiritual self awareness had begun to grow."

In his books published in Taiwan, Master Ni did not give the details of his spiritual background. It was ancient Taoist custom that all writers, such as Lao Tzu and Chuang Tzu, avoided giving their personal description. Lao Tzu and Chuang Tzu were not even their names. However, Master Ni conforms with the modern system of biographies and copyrights to meet the needs of the new society.

Master Ni's teaching differs from what is generally called Taoism in modern times. There is no comparison or relationship between his teaching and conventional folk Taoism. Master Ni describes his independent teaching as having been trained without the narrow concept of lineage or religious mixture of folk Taoism. It is non-conventional and differs from the teaching of any other teachers.

Master Ni shares his own achievement as the teaching of rejuvenated Taoism, which has its origins in the prehistoric stages of human life. Master Ni's teaching is the Integral Way or Integral Taoism. It is based on the Three Scriptures of Taoist Mysticism: Lao Tzu's *Tao Teh Ching*, *The Teachings of Chuang Tzu* and *The I Ching (The Book of Changes)*. Master Ni has translated these three classics into versions which carry the accuracy of the most valuable ancient message. His other books are materials for different stages of learning Tao. He has also absorbed all the truthful and highest spiritual achievements from various schools to assist the illustration of Tao with his own achieved insight on those different levels of teachings.

The ancient Taoist writing contained in the Three Scriptures of Taoist Mysticism and all Taoist books of many schools were very difficult to understand, even for Chinese scholars. Thus, the real Taoist teaching is not known to most scholars of later generations, the Chinese people or foreign translators. It would have become lost to the world if Master Ni, with his spiritual achievement, had not rewritten it and put it into simple language. He has practically revived the ancient teaching to make it useful for all people.

It is the true, traditional spirit of the teaching of Tao, different from some leaders in later times who made it as the mixed Taoist religion. Toward society, the teaching of Tao serves as public spiritual education. Toward individuals, the teaching guides internal spiritual prctice. Therefore, the true teaching of Tao has nothing to do with any religions which use formality and damage the true, independent spirit. Although some traditional practice has some external layout, it is the symbol of spiritual practice and some postures which are for guiding or conducting energy in the body. Since its beginnings, this true tradition of Tao has been independent of social limitation. It has also never been involved with the competition of any social religion because this tradition's goal is to help the spiritual development of individuals, broad human society, all religion and culture. Its spiritual teaching is above the confusion of custom and fashionable thought which happens in the frame of time and location. The teaching of Tao serves a deeper and higher sphere of limited life.

Throughout the world, Master Ni teaches the simple, pure message of his spiritual ancestors to assist modern people understand life and awakening to Tao. Taoist Master Ni, Hua-Ching has spoken out and clearly offered more teaching than any other true Taoist master in history. With his achieved insight, over 80 years of training and teaching, and his deep spiritual commitment, Master Ni shares his own achievement as the pure rejuvenated teaching of the Integral Tao.

BOOKS IN ENGLISH BY MASTER NI

The Key to Good Fortune: Refining Your Spirit - *New Publication!*
A translation of Straighten Your Way (Tai Shan Kan Yin Pien) and The Silent Way of Blessing (Yin Chia Wen), which are the main guidance for a mature and healthy life. This amplified version of the popular booklet called The Heavenly Way includes a new commentary section by Master Ni which discusses how spiritual improvement can become an integral part of one's life and how to realize a Heavenly life on earth. 144 pages. Stock No. BKEYT. Softcover, $12.95

Eternal Light - *New Publication!*
In this book, Master Ni presents the life and teachings of his father, Grandmaster Ni, Yo San, who was a spiritually achieved person, a Taoist healer and teacher, and a source of inspiration to Master Ni in his life. Here is an intimate look at the lifestyle of a spiritual family. Some of the deeper teachings and understandings of spirituality passed from father to son are clearly given and elucidated. This book is recommended for those committed to living a spiritual way of life and wishing for higher achievement. 208 pages Stock No. BETER Softcover, $14.95

Quest of Soul - *New Publication!*
In Quest of Soul, Master Ni addresses many subjects relevant to understanding one's own soul, such as the religious concept of saving the soul, how to improve the quality of the personal soul, the high spiritual achievement of free soul, what happens spiritually at death and the universal soul. He guides the reader into deeper knowledge of oneself and inspires each individual to move forward to increase both one's own personal happiness and spiritual level. 152 pages. Stock No. BQUES Softcover, $11.95

Nurture Your Spirits - New Publication!
With truthful spiritual knowledge, you have better life attitudes that are more supportive to your existence. With truthful spiritual knowledge, nobody can cause you spiritual confusion. Where can you find such advantage? It would take a lifetime of development in a correct school, but such a school is not available. However, in this book, Master Ni breaks some spiritual prohibitions and presents the spiritual truth he has studied and proven. This truth may help you develop and nurture your own spirits, which are the truthful internal foundation of your life being. Taoism is educational; its purpose is not to group people and build social strength but to help each individual build one's own spiritual strength. 176 pages. Stock No. BNURT Softcover, $12.95

Internal Growth Through Tao - New Publication!
Material goods can be passed from one person to another, but growth and awareness cannot be given in the same way. Spiritual development is related to one's own internal and external beingness. Through books, discussion or classes, wise people are able to use others' experiences to kindle their own inner light to help their own

growth and live a life of no separation from their own spiritual nature. In this book, Master Ni teaches the more subtle, much deeper sphere of the reality of life that is above the shallow sphere of external achievement. He also shows the confusion caused by some spiritual teachings and guides you in the direction of developing spiritually by growing internally. 208 pages. Stock No. BINTE Softcover, $13.95

Power of Natural Healing - New Publication!
Master Ni discusses the natural capability of self-healing in this book, which is healing physical trouble untreated by medication or external measure. He offers information and practices which can assist any treatment method currently being used by someone seeking health. He goes deeper to discuss methods of Taoist cultivation which promote a healthy life, including Taoist spiritual achievement, which brings about health and longevity. This book is not only suitable for a person seeking to improve one's health condition. Those who wish to live long and happy, and to understand more about living a natural healthy lifestyle, may be supported by the practice of Taoist energy cultivation. 230 pages. Stock No. BPOWE Softcover, $14.95

Essence of Universal Spirituality
In this volume, as an open-minded learner and achieved teacher of universal spirituality, Master Ni examines and discusses all levels and topics of religious and spiritual teaching to help you develop your own correct knowledge of the essence existing above the differences in religious practice. He reviews religious teachings with hope to benefit modern people. This book is to help readers to come to understand the ultimate truth and enjoy the achievement of all religions without becoming confused by them. 304 pages. Stock No. BESSE Softcover, $19.95

Guide to Inner Light
Modern life is controlled by city environments, cultural customs, religious teachings and politics that can all divert our attention away from our natural life being. As a result, we lose the perspective of viewing ourselves as natural completeness. This book reveals the development of ancient Taoist adepts. Drawing inspiration from their experience, modern people looking for the true source and meaning of life can find great teachings to direct and benefit them. The invaluable ancient Taoist development can teach us to reach the attainable spiritual truth and point the way to the Inner Light. Master Ni uses the ancient high accomplishments to make this book a useful resource. 192 pages. Stock No. BGUID. Softcover, $12.95

Stepping Stones for Spiritual Success
In Asia, the custom of foot binding was followed for almost a thousand years. In the West, people did not bind feet, but they bound their thoughts for a much longer period, some 1,500 to 1,700 years. Their mind and thinking became unnatural. Being un-natural expresses a state of confusion where people do not know what is right. Once they become natural again, they are clear and progress is great. Master Ni invites his

readers to unbind their minds; in this volume, he has taken the best of the traditional teachings and put them into contemporary language to make them more relevant to our time, culture and lives. 160 pages. Stock No. BSTEP. Softcover, $12.95.

The Complete Works of Lao Tzu
Lao Tzu's Tao Teh Ching is one of the most widely translated and cherished works of literature in the world. It presents the core of Taoist philosophy. Lao Tzu's timeless wisdom provides a bridge to subtle spiritual truth and practical guidelines for harmonious and peaceful living. Master Ni includes what is believed to be the only English translation of the Hua Hu Ching, a later work of Lao Tzu which has been lost to the general public for a thousand years. 212 pages. Stock No. BCOMP. Softcover, $12.95

Order The Complete Works of Lao Tzu and the companion Tao Teh Ching Cassette Tapes for only $25.00. Stock No. ABTAO.

The Book of Changes and the Unchanging Truth
The first edition of this book was widely appreciated by its readers, who drew great spiritual benefit from it. They found the principles of the I Ching to be clearly explained and useful to their lives, especially the commentaries. The legendary classic I Ching is recognized as mankind's first written book of wisdom. Leaders and sages throughout history have consulted it as a trusted advisor to reveal appropriate action to be taken in any of life's circumstances. This volume also includes over 200 pages of of material on Taoist principles of natural energy cycles, instruction and commentaries. New, revised second edition, 669 pages. Stock No. BBOOK. Hardcover, $35.95

The Story of Two Kingdoms
This volume is the metaphoric tale of the conflict between the Kingdoms of Light and Darkness. Through this unique story, Master Ni transmits the esoteric teachings of Taoism which have been carefully guarded secrets for over 5,000 years. This book is for those who are serious in their search and have devoted their lives to achieving high spiritual goals. 122 pages. Stock No. BSTOR. Hardcover, $14.95

The Way of Integral Life
This book can help build a bridge for those wishing to connect spiritual and intellectual development. It is most helpful for modern educated people. It includes practical and applicable suggestions for daily life, philosophical thought, esoteric insight and guidelines for those aspiring to give help and service to the world. This book helps you learn the wisdom of the ancient sages' achievement to assist the growth of your own wisdom and integrate it as your own new light and principles for balanced, reasonable living in worldly life. 320 pages. Softcover, $14.95, Stock No. BWAYS. Hardcover, $20.95, Stock No. BWAYH

Enlightenment: Mother of Spiritual Independence

The inspiring story and teachings of Master Hui Neng, the father of Zen Buddhism and Sixth Patriarch of the Buddhist tradition, highlight this volume. Hui Neng was a person of ordinary birth, intellectually unsophisticated, who achieved himself to become a spiritual leader. Master Ni includes enlivening commentaries and explanations of the principles outlined by this spiritual revolutionary. Having received the same training as all Zen Masters as one aspect of his training and spiritual achievement, Master Ni offers this teaching to guide his readers in their process of spiritual development. 264 pages. Softcover, $12.95, Stock No. BENLS. Hardcover, $18.95, Stock No. BENLH

Attaining Unlimited Life

The thought-provoking teachings of Chuang Tzu are presented in this volume. He was perhaps the greatest philosopher and master of Taoism and he laid the foundation for the Taoist school of thought. Without his work, people of later generations would hardly recognize the value of Lao Tzu's teaching in practical, everyday life. He touches the organic nature of human life more deeply and directly than that of other great teachers. This volume also includes questions by students and answers by Master Ni. 467 pages. Softcover, $18.95, Stock No. BATTS; Hardcover, $25.95, Stock No. BATTH

The Gentle Path of Spiritual Progress

This book offers a glimpse into the dialogues of a Taoist master and his students. In a relaxed, open manner, Master Ni, Hua-Ching explains to his students the fundamental practices that are the keys to experiencing enlightenment in everyday life. Many of the traditional secrets of Taoist training are revealed. His students also ask a surprising range of questions, and Master Ni's answers touch on contemporary psychology, finances, sexual advice, how to use the I Ching as well as the telling of some fascinating Taoist legends. Softcover, $12.95, Stock No. BGENT

Spiritual Messages from a Buffalo Rider, A Man of Tao

This is another important collection of Master Ni's service in his worldly trip, originally published as one half of The Gentle Path. He had the opportunity to meet people and answer their questions to help them gain the spiritual awareness that we live at the command of our animal nature. Our buffalo nature rides on us, whereas an achieved person rides the buffalo. In this book, Master Ni gives much helpful knowledge to those who are interested in improving their lives and deepening their cultivation so they too can develop beyond their mundane beings. Softcover, $12.95, Stock No. BSPIR

8,000 Years of Wisdom, Volume I and II

This two volume set contains a wealth of practical, down-to-earth advice given by Master Ni to his students over a five year period, 1979 to 1983. Drawing on his training in Traditional Chinese Medicine, Herbology, Acupuncture and other Taoist arts, Master Ni gives candid answers to students' questions on many topics ranging from dietary guidance to sex and pregnancy, meditation techniques and natural cures for common illnesses. Volume I includes dietary guidance; 236 pages; Stock No. BWIS1 Volume II includes sex and pregnancy guidance; 241 pages; Stock No. BWIS2. Softcover, Each Volume $12.95

The Uncharted Voyage Towards the Subtle Light

Spiritual life in the world today has become a confusing mixture of dying traditions and radical novelties. People who earnestly and sincerely seek something more than just a way to fit into the complexities of a modern structure that does not support true self-development often find themselves spiritually struggling. This book provides a profound understanding and insight into the underlying heart of all paths of spiritual growth, the subtle origin and the eternal truth of one universal life. 424 pages. Stock No. BUNCH. Softcover, $14.95

The Heavenly Way

A translation of the classic Tai Shan Kan Yin Pien (Straighten Your Way) and Yin Chia Wen (The Silent Way of Blessing). The treaties in this booklet are the main guidance for a mature and healthy life. The purpose of this booklet is to promote the recognition of truth, because only truth can teach the perpetual Heavenly Way by which one reconnects oneself with the divine nature. 41 pages. Stock No. BHEAV. Softcover, $2.95

Footsteps of the Mystical Child

This book poses and answers such questions as: What is a soul? What is wisdom? What is spiritual evolution? The answers to these and many other questions enable readers to open themselves to new realms of understanding and personal growth. There are also many true examples about people's internal and external struggles on the path of self-development and spiritual evolution. 166 pages. Stock No. BFOOT. Softcover, $9.95

Workbook for Spiritual Development

This book offers a practical, down-to-earth, hands-on approach for those who are devoted to the path of spiritual achievement. The reader will find diagrams showing fundamental hand positions to increase and channel one's spiritual energy, postures for sitting, standing and sleeping cultivation as well as postures for many Taoist invocations. The material in this workbook is drawn from the traditional teachings of Taoism and summarizes thousands of years of little known practices for spiritual development. An entire section is devoted to ancient invocations, another on natural celibacy and another on postures. In addition, Master Ni explains the basic attitudes and understandings that are the foundation for Taoist practices. 224 pages. Stock No. BWORK. Softcover, $12.95

Poster of Master Lu

Color poster of Master Lu, Tung Ping (shown on cover of workbook), for use with the workbook or in one's shrine. 16" x 22"; Stock No. PMLTP. $10.95

The Taoist Inner View of the Universe

This presentation of Taoist metaphysics provides guidance for one's own personal life transformation. Master Ni has given all the opportunity to know the vast achievement of the ancient unspoiled mind and its transpiercing vision. This book offers a glimpse of the inner world and immortal realm known to achieved Taoists and makes it understandable for students aspiring to a more complete life. 218 pages. Stock No. BTAOI. Softcover, $12.95

Tao, the Subtle Universal Law

Most people are unaware that their thoughts and behavior evoke responses from the invisible net of universal energy. The real meaning of Taoist self-discipline is to harmonize with universal law. To lead a good stable life is to be aware of the actual conjoining of the universal subtle law with every moment of our lives. This book presents the wisdom and practical methods that the ancient Chinese have successfully used for centuries to accomplish this. 165 pages. Stock No. TAOS. Softcover, $7.95

MATERIALS ON TAOIST HEALTH, ARTS AND SCIENCES

BOOKS

The Tao of Nutrition by Maoshing Ni, Ph.D., with Cathy McNease, B.S., M.H. - Working from ancient Chinese medical classics and contemporary research, Dr. Maoshing Ni and Cathy McNease have compiled an indispensable guide to natural healing. This exceptional book shows the reader how to take control of one's health through one's eating habits. This volume contains 3 major sections: the first section deals with theories of Chinese nutrition and philosophy; the second describes over 100 common foods in detail, listing their energetic properties, therapeutic actions and individual remedies. The third section lists nutritional remedies for many common ailments. This book presents both a healing system and a disease prevention system which is flexible in adapting to every individual's needs. 214 pages. Stock No. BNUTR. Softcover, $14.95

Chinese Vegetarian Delights by Lily Chuang
An extraordinary collection of recipes based on principles of traditional Chinese nutrition. Many recipes are therapeutically prepared with herbs. Diet has long been recognized as a key factor in health and longevity. For those who require restricted diets and those who choose an optimal diet, this cookbook is a rare treasure. Meat, sugar, diary products and fried foods are excluded. Produce, grains, tofu, eggs and seaweeds are imaginatively prepared. 104 pages. Stock No. BCHIV. Softcover, $7.95

Chinese Herbology Made Easy - by Maoshing Ni, Ph.D.
This text provides an overview of Oriental medical theory, in-depth descriptions of each herb category, with over 300 black and white photographs, extensive tables of individual herbs for easy reference, and an index of pharmaceutical and Pin-Yin names. The distillation of overwhelming material into essential elements enables one to focus efficiently and develop a clear understanding of Chinese herbology. This book is especially helpful for those studying for their California Acupuncture License. 202 pages. Stock No. BCHIH. Softcover, 14.95

Crane Style Chi Gong Book - By Daoshing Ni, Ph.D.
Chi Gong is a set of meditative exercises that was developed several thousand years ago by Taoists in China. It is now practiced for healing purposes, combining breathing techniques, body movements and mental imagery to guide the smooth flow of energy throughout the body. This book gives a more detailed account and study of Chi Gong than the videotape alone. It may be used with or without the videotape. Includes complete instructions and information on using Chi Gong exercise as a medical therapy. 55 pages. Stock No. BCRAN. Spiral bound $10.95

Physical Movement for Spiritual Learning: Dao-In Physical Art for a Long and Happy Life (VHS) - by Master Ni.
Dao-In is a series of typical Taoist movements which are traditionally used for physical energy conducting. These exercises were passed down from the ancient achieved Taoists and immortals. The ancients discovered that Dao-In exercises not only solved problems of stagnant energy, but also increased their health and lengthened their years. The exercises are also used as practical support for cultivation and the higher achievements of spiritual immortality. Master Ni, Hua-Ching, heir to the tradition of the achieved masters, is the first one who releases this important Taoist practice to the modern world in this 1 hour videotape. VHS $59.95

T'ai Chi Chuan: An Appreciation *(VHS) - by Master Ni*
Different styles of T'ai Chi Ch'uan as Movement have different purposes and accomplish different results. In this long awaited videotape, Master Ni, Hua-Ching presents three styles of T'ai Chi Movement handed down to him through generations of highly developed masters. They are the "Gentle Path," "Sky Journey," and "Infinite Expansion" styles of T'ai Chi Movement. The three styles are presented uninterrupted in this unique videotape and are set to music for observation and appreciation. VHS 30 minutes $49.95

Crane Style Chi Gong *(VHS) - by Dr. Daoshing Ni, Ph.D.*
Chi Gong is a set of meditative exercises developed several thousand years ago by ancient Taoists in China. It is now practiced for healing stubborn chronic diseases, strengthening the body to prevent disease and as a tool for further spiritual enlightenment. It combines breathing techniques, simple body movements, and mental imagery to guide the smooth flow of energy throughout the body. Chi gong is easy to learn for all ages. Correct and persistent practice will increase one's energy, relieve stress or tension, improve concentration and clarity, release emotional stress and restore general well-being. 2 hours Stock No. VCRAN. $65.95

Eight Treasures *(VHS) - By Maoshing Ni, Ph.D.*
These exercises help open blocks in a person's energy flow and strengthen one's vitality. It is a complete exercise combining physical stretching and toning and energy conducting movements coordinated with breathing. The Eight Treasures are an exercise unique to the Ni family. Patterned from nature, the 32 movements of the Eight Treasures are an excellent foundation for Tai Chi Chuan or martial arts. 1 hour and 45 minutes. Stock No. VEIGH. $49.95

Tai Chi Chuan I & II *(VHS) - By Maoshing Ni, Ph.D.*
This exercise integrates the flow of physical movement with that of integral energy in the Taoist style of "Harmony," similar to the long form of Yang-style Tai Chi Chuan. Tai Chi has been practiced for thousands of years to help both physical longevity and spiritual cultivation. 1 hour each. Each Video Tape $49.95. Order both for $90.00. Stock Nos: Part I, VTAI1; Part II, VTAI2; Set of two, VTAI3.

AUDIO CASSETTES

Invocations: Health and Longevity and Healing a Broken Heart - By Maoshing Ni, Ph.D.
This audio cassette guides the listener through a series of ancient invocations to channel and conduct one's own healing energy and vital force. "Thinking is louder than thunder." The mystical power by which all miracles are brought about is your sincere practice of this principle. 30 minutes. Stock No. AINVO. $5.95

Chi Gong for Stress Release - By Maoshing Ni, Ph.D.
This audio cassette guides you through simple, ancient breathing exercises that enable you to release day-to-day stress and tension that are such a common cause of illness today. 30 minutes. Stock No. ACHIS. $8.95

Chi Gong for Pain Management - By Maoshing Ni, Ph.D.
Using easy visualization and deep-breathing techniques that have been developed over thousands of years, this audio cassette offers methods for overcoming pain by invigorating your energy flow and unblocking obstructions that cause pain. 30 minutes. Stock No. ACHIP. $8.95

Tao Teh Ching Cassette Tapes
This classic work of Lao Tzu has been recorded in this two-cassette set that is a companion to the book translated by Master Ni. Professionally recorded and read by Robert Rudelson. 120 minutes. Stock No. ATAOT. $15.95

Order Master Ni's book, The Complete Works of Lao Tzu, and Tao Teh Ching Cassette Tapes for only $25.00. Stock No. ABTAO.

Many people write or call asking for information on how to set up study groups or centers in their own community. To respond to such requests, the Center for Taoist Arts in Atlanta, Georgia has offered to show others how they have set up their own center and discussion group. If you are interested, please contact Frank Gibson, The Center for Taoist Arts, PO Box 1389, Alpharetta, GA 30239-1389.

How To Order

Complete this form and mail it to: **Union of Tao and Man,**
117 Stonehaven Way, Los Angeles, CA 90049 (213)-472-9970

Name: _____

Address: _____

City: _____ State: _____ Zip: _____

Phone - Daytime: _____ Evening: _____

(We may telephone you if we have questions about your order.)

Qty.	Stock No.	Title/Description	Price Each	Total Price

Total amount for items ordered _____

Sales tax (CA residents, 6-1/2%) _____

Shipping Charge (See below) _____

Total Amount Enclosed _____

Please allow 6 - 8 weeks for delivery.
Thank you for your order.

U. S. Funds Only, Please
Please write your check or money order
to Union of Tao and Man

Shipping Charge - All Orders Sent Via U.S. Postal Service, unless specified.
Domestic Surface Mail: First item $2.00, each additional, add $.50.
Canada/Mexico Surface Mail: First item $2.50, each additional, add $1.00.
Other Foreign Surface Mail: First Item $3.00, each additional, add $2.00.
Foreign Air Mail: First item $18.00, each additional, add $7.00.

Credit Card orders only: **VISA**   **MasterCard**
☐ Visa   ☐ MasterCard
(13 or 16 digits)   (16 digits)

Card Account Number
| | | | | | | | | | | | | | | | |
1 2 3 4 5 6 7 8 9 10 11 12 13 14 15 16

Expiration Date of Card [ ] [ ] — [ ] [ ]

Signature: _____

Spiritual Study Through the College of Tao

The College of Tao and the Union of Tao and Man were established formally in California in the 1970's. This tradition is a very old spiritual culture of mankind, holding long experience of human spiritual growth. Its central goal is to offer healthy spiritual education to all people of our society. This time tested tradition values the spiritual development of each individual self and passes down its guidance and experience.

Master Ni carries his tradition from its country of origin to the west. He chooses to avoid making the mistake of old-style religions that have rigid establishments which resulted in fossilizing the delicacy of spiritual reality. Rather, he prefers to guide the teachings of his tradition as a school of no boundary rather than a religion with rigidity. Thus, the branches or centers of this Taoist school offer different programs of similar purpose. Each center extends its independent service, but all are unified in adopting Master Ni's work as the foundation of teaching to fulfill the mission of providing spiritual education to all people.

The centers offer their classes, teaching, guidance and practices on building the groundwork for cultivating a spiritually centered and well-balanced life. As a person obtains the correct knowledge with which to properly guide himself or herself, he or she can then become more skillful in handling the experiences of daily life. The assimilation of good guidance in one's practical life brings about different stages of spiritual development.

Any interested individual is welcome to join and learn to grow for oneself. You might like to join the center near where you live, or you yourself may be interested in organizing a center or study group based on the model of existing centers. In that way, we all work together for the spiritual benefit of all people. We do not require any religious type of commitment.

The learning is life. The development is yours. The connection of study may be helpful, useful and serviceable, directly to you.

- -

Mail to: Union of Tao and Man, 117 Stonehaven Way, Los Angeles, CA 90049

_____ I wish to be put on the mailing list of the Union of Tao and Man to be notified of classes, educational activities and new publications.

Name:_____

Address:_____

City:_____State:_____Zip:_____

This list of Master Ni's books in English is ordered by date of publication for those readers who wish to follow the sequence of his Western teaching material in their learning of Tao.

1979: *The Complete Works of Lao Tzu*
The Taoist Inner View of the Universe
Tao, the Subtle Universal Law
1981: *The Heavenly Way*
1983: *The Book of Changes and the Unchanging Truth*
8,000 Years of Wisdom, I
8,000 Years of Wisdom, II
1984: *Workbook for Spiritual Development*
1985: *The Uncharted Voyage Towards the Subtle Light*
1986: *Footsteps of the Mystical Child*
1987: *The Gentle Path of Spiritual Progress*
Spiritual Messages from a Buffalo Rider, (originally part of *Gentle Path of Spiritual Progress*)
1989: *The Way of Integral Life*
Enlightenment: Mother of Spiritual Independence
Attaining Unlimited Life
The Story of Two Kingdoms
1990: *Stepping Stones for Spiritual Success*
Guide to Inner Light
Essence of Universal Spirituality
1991: *Internal Growth through Tao*
Nurture Your Spirits
Quest of Soul
Power of Natural Healing
Attune Your Body with Dao-In: Taoist Exercise for a Long and Happy Life
Eternal Light
Harmony: The Art of Life
The Key to Good Fortune: Refining Your Spirit
The Cloudless Sky: Cleanse Your Emotion and Achieve Spiritually

In addition, the forthcoming books will be compiled from his lecturing and teaching service:

Golden Message (by Daoshing and Maoshing Ni, based on the works of Master Ni, Hua-Ching)
A Guide to Learning Sky Journey T'ai Chi Chuan
A Guide to Learning Infinite Expansion T'ai Chi Chuan
A Guide to Learning Cosmic Tour Ba Gua
The Mystical Universal Mother: The Teachings of Mother of Yellow Altar

Herbs Used by Ancient Taoist Masters

The pursuit of everlasting youth or immortality throughout human history is an innate human desire. Long ago, Chinese esoteric Taoists went to the high mountains to contemplated nature, strengthen their bodies, empower their minds and develop their spirit. From their studies and cultivation, they gave China alchemy and chemistry, herbology and acupuncture, the I Ching, astrology, martial arts and T'ai Chi Chuan, Chi Gong and many other useful kinds of knowledge.

Most important, they handed down in secrecy methods for attaining longevity and spiritual immortality. There were different levels of approach; one was to use a collection of food herb formulas that were only available to highly achieved Taoist masters. They used these food herbs to increase energy and heighten vitality. This treasured collection of herbal formulas remained within the Ni family for centuries.

Now, through Traditions of Tao, the Ni family makes these foods available for you to use to assist the foundation of your own positive development. It is only with a strong foundation that expected results are produced from diligent cultivation.

As a further benefit, in concert with the Taoist principle of self-sufficiency, Traditions of Tao offers the food herbs along with the Union of Tao and Man's publications in a distribution opportunity for anyone serious about financial independence.

Send to: *Traditions of Tao*
              c/o 117 Stonehaven Way
              Los Angeles, CA 90049

☐ *Please send me a Traditions of Tao brochure.*

☐ *Please send me information on becoming an independent distributor of Traditions of Tao herbal products and publications.*

Name _____

Address _____

City _____ *State* _____ *Zip* _____

Phone (day) _____ *(night)* _____

Yo San University of Traditional Chinese Medicine

"Not just a medical career, but a life-time commitment to raising one's spiritual standard."

Thank you for your support and interest in our publications and services. It is by your patronage that we continue to offer you the practical knowledge and wisdom from this venerable Taoist tradition.

Because of your sustained interest in Taoism, we formed Yo San University of Traditional Chinese Medicine, a non-profit educational institute in January 1989 under the direction of founder Master Ni, Hua-Ching. Yo San University is the continuation of 38 generations of Ni family practitioners who handed down knowledge and wisdom from fathers to sons. Its purpose is to train and graduate practitioners of the highest caliber in Traditional Chinese Medicine, which includes acupuncture, herbology and spiritual development.

We view Traditional Chinese Medicine as the application of spiritual development. Its foundation is the spiritual capability to know life, to know a person's problem and how to cure it. We teach students how to care for themselves and others, and emphasize the integration of traditional knowledge and modern science. We offer a complete Master's degree program approved by the California State Department of Education that provides an excellent education in Traditional Chinese Medicine and meets all requirements for state licensure.

We invite you to inquire into our school about a creative and rewarding career as a holistic physician. Classes are also open to persons interested only in self-enrichment. For more information, please fill out the form below and send it to:

Yo San University,
12304 Santa Monica Blvd. Suite 104,
Los Angeles, CA 90025

☐ Please send me information on the Masters degree program in Traditional Chinese Medicine.

☐ Please send me information on health workshops and seminars.

☐ Please send me information on continuing education for acupuncturists and health professionals.

Name _____

Address _____

City_____ State_____ Zip_____

Phone(day)_____ (night)_____

INDEX
Of Selected Topics